MATTHEW HALY'S

book of UPHOLSTERY

MATTHEW HALY'S
book of UPHOLSTERY

PROJECTS, TIPS, TRICKS, AND TECHNIQUES

MATTHEW HALY

WITH

Kathleen Hackett

POTTER
CRAFT

NEW YORK

Copyright © 2008 by Matthew Haly
Photographs and illustrations copyright © 2008 by Potter Craft,
an imprint of the Crown Publishing Group, a division of Random House, Inc.

Published in the United States by Potter Craft, an imprint of the Crown Publishing Group,
a division of Random House, Inc., New York.
www.crownpublishing.com
www.pottercraft.com

POTTER CRAFT and colophon is a registered trademark of Random House, Inc.

Library of Congress Cataloging-in-Publication Data

Haly, Matthew.
Matthew Haly's book of upholstery : projects, tips, tricks, and techniques / Matthew Haly
with Kathleen Hackett.—1st ed.
p.   cm.
Includes index.
ISBN-13: 978-0-307-40567-8
1. Upholstery—Amateurs' manuals.   2. Slip covers—Amateurs' manuals.   I. Title:
Book of upholstery.   II. Hackett, Kathleen.   III. Title.
TT198.H244   2008
746.9'5—dc22   2008007197

ISBN: 978-0-307-40567-8

Printed in China

Design by Susi Oberhelman
Photographs by Marcus Tullis
Illustrations by Woolypear
Photos on pages 19, 65, 125, 187, and 188 courtesy of Amy Sly
Photos on pages 190, 192, and 193 courtesy of Ksenya Samarskaya

1   3   5   7   9   10   8   6   4   2

First Edition

Special thanks to the following fabric companies who generously
donated fabrics and trimming for the projects in the book:

Clarence House

Cowtan & Tout

Hinson & Company

Larsen

Lulu DK at Hinson & Company

M & J Trimming

Manuel Canovas

Scalamandré

Old World Weavers

*Jaden,
welcome
to the
world*

CONTENTS

INTRODUCTION

Twenty-five years ago, as a teenager growing up in Hamilton, New Zealand, if anyone had suggested that I would one day own and operate a thriving upholstery business in New York City, I would have responded the way I did to most career predictions back then. *Bollocks*, I would say. After all, if one took stock of my resume up to that point— a fondness for wood shop, tennis, boxing, and playing the electric guitar in a punk rock band and a dislike for sitting in classrooms—there was little indication that my future involved being called on by interior designers, shelter magazines, celebrities, and design-minded homeowners to produce upholstered pieces for perfectionist clients and sophisticated readers.

In truth, there were auspicious signs. My first job, at fourteen, was at a local sewing factory where, one month into it, the boss suggested I might be well-suited for a position at his upholsterer-friend's studio. For three weeks straight, I sat on a tiny stool in front of a machine, sanding chair legs. Eager to move on from my miniscule seat, I suggested to the boss that he make me his apprentice, but to no avail. His denial was actually a gift: I rotated around his shop and gained an in-depth knowledge of the foundations of upholstery: frames, foam, batting, webbing—you name it.

Romantic it was not, and for that reason, at sixteen, I set my sights on Australia. What began as a couple weeks of holiday turned into a four-year stay in Orange, New South Wales. There, I worked in a variety of jobs, including landscaping, picking apples, working in a glass factory, and kneading dough in a commercial bakery. Though I loved working with my hands, the odd jobs made me restless, so I decided to move to Canada, where I was born, to pursue my musical aspirations. In between practicing and touring, I again took various jobs—picking tobacco and selling clothing among them— including one of the most demanding of my life, working with troubled youth. No matter how rewarding a job was, though, I always eagerly returned to upholstery,

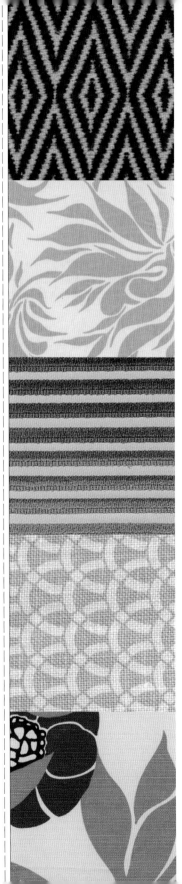

working in several dozen studios in and around Toronto. With each stint, I grew more and more adept at the art of it, especially when it came to hand-making frames and cutting fabric. I eventually settled in New York City, lured by a record deal and anchored by an unfulfilling though successful real estate career.

The problem was I hated selling. Whether it was clothing or co-ops, I realized that I wasn't comfortable as a pitchman, that putting my hands to work was infinitely more rewarding. Thus The Furniture Joint was born. Out of a vest-pocket–sized storefront in Manhattan's East Village, I restored, reupholstered, and sold furniture. Rather than waiting for customers to bring their tired pieces to me, I plied antique shops and estate sales every weekend, picking up items most people considered junk and bringing them back to life. Within weeks of opening the doors, customers began asking me to reupholster their own pieces. Just eight months later, my upholstery business was booming. The demand for it was high—and so was the price. After I turned away dozens of customers who couldn't afford the upholstery they wanted, I decided to offer classes so that they could learn how to do it themselves. From the day I announced the courses, I've had a running waiting list fifty names deep.

Call it an outgrowth of the DIY craze or simply a desire to restore beauty to a haggard piece of furniture, but the act of transforming something with your own hands is compelling enough a reason, I think, to work your way through the projects in this book. Though nine out of ten of my students bound into my classes with visions of reupholstering a sofa in their favorite fabric as their first project, the curriculum is designed foremost to foster confidence in the foundations of upholstery. Putting the fabric on, I tell them, is the icing on the cake. If you don't begin with an expertly rendered foundation, not even the most forgiving or pricey fabric will look good.

With that philosophy in mind, I have organized these projects into straightforward categories of Easy, Intermediate, and Advanced. If you are new to upholstery and/or sewing, the Easy chapter is designed to make you comfortable with measuring, marking, and cutting fabric, as well as using a sewing machine. Simple pillows, a table runner, and a lampshade are some examples of the items that emphasize these basics. Once you've mastered these, hone your measuring skills by making the lined round tablecloth, then embark on your first upholstered piece, a stool with French nails. In the Intermediate chapter, you will learn how to make a box cushion with a zipper, a project well worth mastering since it is among the most common seats on sofas and chairs. The world of windows is covered in this chapter, with lessons in making full-length curtains, a Roman shade, and a cornice. As always, measuring is a primary focus, as is working with foam padding. Decorative stitching, including French-stitching and biscuit tufting, are hallmarks of the Advanced chapter, as are making a full-length slipcover for one chair and fully upholstering another.

Wherever you begin, keep in mind that though I've adapted all of the projects to accommodate a home upholsterer, I haven't oversimplified, cheated methods, or cut corners for the sake of making them appear easy. My goal is to teach upholstery skills that are used by the professionals—and to dispel any notion you may have gotten from DIY television that upholstering is a snap. Indeed, to do it right, reupholstering requires time and patience. And more patience. And more patience after that. Even after twenty-one years in the business, and with a 4,300-square-foot studio, several employees, and every tool imaginable at my fingertips, I am still learning. There is one thing, however, that I can say with certainty: Creating something with your hands and taking pride in its craftsmanship is the most satisfying part of it all.

GETTING STARTED

From the day that I began offering upholstery classes seven years ago, I have found myself repeating several basic tenets of upholstery to such an extent that they now sound more like mantras. The truth is, no matter how seasoned you become as an upholsterer, you can never be reminded enough about such things as tension, measuring, and cutting.

1. Measure twice, cut once.
2. Measure all of the elements of the piece, including the height of the seat from the floor.
3. Take an excessive number of pictures as you strip the frame.
4. Keeping the tension of the fabric consistent is key.
5. All upholstery fabric should be smoothed over the piece with your hands, not tugged or pulled tight, to achieve a relaxed fit.
6. Take fabric cues from the upholstery you are replacing. For example, a curved chair (think those mid-century modern egg-shaped chairs) is not a good candidate for a patterned or striped fabric, because the curves of the chair distort the design on the fabric.
7. The real work is on the inside: A solid foundation of webbing, foam, and Dacron® ensures that your piece will hold up.
8. Be realistic about your upholstering goals. Work up to the hard stuff.
9. Have a partner, as well as music.
10. A good upholsterer never blames his tools!

There's obviously more to upholstering than this, but I guarantee that after completing one or two projects, you will find yourself coming back to these ten phrases over and over. However, before starting even a simple project, please read **The Language of Upholstery** (page 177) and **Upholstery Techniques 101** (page 186). Familiarizing yourself now with this essential information on the supplies, tools, and techniques of upholstery will help immensely when making the projects.

BASIC UPHOLSTERY TOOLS

The following is a list of the most common tools you will need for the projects in this book.

Dressmaker's pins

Dressmaker's tape measure

Drill

Electric staple gun and staples

Heavy duty shears

Hot glue gun and glue

Iron

Metal ruler/yardstick

Pencil

Permanent marker

Regulator

Rubber mallet

Screwdriver

School chalk

Seam ripper

Sewing machine

Square

Staple remover

Tacking hammer

Thread

Tufting needle
(for pulling out corners)

Upholstery pins

Upholstery tacks
(for temporary "pinning")

Webbing stretcher

Wire brush (for scraping old glue away)

Wooden yardstick

easy

Call it providence—or perhaps the wisdom of a disciplinarian dad—but my entrée into the working world, as an assistant at a sewing factory, seems to have set me on the course for my life's work in upholstery. Likewise, if you are going to become an accomplished at-home upholsterer, the first step is to become comfortable measuring and cutting accurately and then working with your sewing machine. How? The obvious answer is through practice. There is no better incentive to heed the mantra "measure twice, cut once" than avoiding the inaccurate measurements that cause an ill-fitting piece.

Working on a scrap piece of fabric first helps avoid making expensive measuring and cutting mistakes. Likewise, using a practice piece of fabric is how my students learn to handle a sewing machine, which is a bit like working with bread dough—you need to get a feel for it, how it responds to varying conditions (fabric types and weights and tension) and how best to work with it under those conditions. One of the first lessons my students learn is how to sew a straight line on the sewing machine. While this may seem like a silly exercise, stitching a straight line at a consistent tension is the key to creating professional-quality upholstered pieces.

In this chapter, I include projects designed to build your confidence—on the cutting table and with the sewing machine. If you are brand new to the world of upholstery, begin at the beginning with a simple lampshade that requires a little measuring, cutting, and sewing. Build on what you've learned by making pillows in which achieving crisp corners is the goal, and then add a box cushion—the building block for sofas and chairs—to your repertoire. You'll also learn hand-stitching, another invaluable upholstery skill, and will employ this technique to close the seams in a round tablecloth and in a pad for a loveseat.

The beauty of the projects in this chapter is that they not only give a beginner a solid grounding in basic upholstery techniques, but also provide the more seasoned among you with useful, beautiful ideas for enhancing the decor in your home.

PATTERNED *lamp*SHADE

USE UPHOLSTERY FABRIC to turn a plain coolie shade—that is, one with a conical shape—into one with decorator quality. Make it easy on yourself by sticking to fabrics with small, repeating prints; large motifs require twice as much fabric and painstaking matching to achieve professional results. For an even easier version of this shade slipcover, use a drum shade instead: You need only cut one piece of fabric in a simple rectangle and machine-sew one seam.

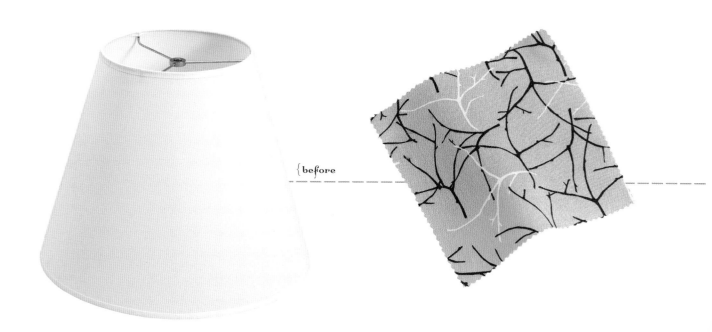

{ before

MATERIALS

- 1 yd (91cm) upholstery-weight fabric
- Dressmaker's tape measure
- Metal ruler
- School chalk
- Dressmaker's pins
- Machine-stitching thread in a complementary color
- Glue gun
- Glue sticks

FINISHED MEASUREMENTS

- All materials are for a 9" high lampshade with a 22" (60cm) diameter at the bottom. Adjust according to the size of your shade.

<<< TIP

Before settling on a fabric, make sure you like the way it looks when light shines through it. The pattern you loved in the store may become obscured or overwhelmed by the grain of the fabric (often the case with patterned linen) when you hold it up to the light.

Measure the Shade

1. Measure the circumference of both the top and bottom of your lampshade using a dressmaker's measuring tape. With a metal ruler, measure the height of the shade, keeping the ruler vertical, not slanted. Our shade measures 42" (106.5cm) around on top, 44" (112cm) around on the bottom, and 9" (23cm) from top to bottom.

2. Determine dimensions for 2 bell shapes, as if your lampshade were cut in half vertically and the pieces flattened out. These will be cut from the upholstery fabric and stitched together with 2 seams. To determine the measurements for the top and bottom of your bells, divide each circumference by 2, then add 1" (2.5cm) (two ½" [13mm] seam allowances). For a shade measuring 42" (106.5cm) around the top and 44" (112cm) around the bottom like ours, the bells should measure 22" (56cm) on top and 23" (58.5cm) on the bottom, including seam allowances.

Prepare the Fabric

3. Lay the upholstery fabric right side up on a work surface, arranging it with the selvedges at your left and right and the cut edges at the top and bottom. Trim the selvedges off. Using a metal ruler and school chalk and working just beneath the top cut edge, mark the fabric with 2 dots to

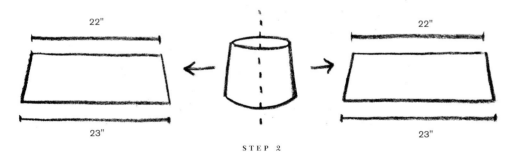

STEP 2

delineate the width of the top bell measure. Ours were 22" (56cm) apart. Mark a dot in the center of these two dots. To mark the bottom edge, measure the height from this center dot (our height was 9" [23cm]). Mark another dot; this will be the center of the bottom edge. The distance between the bottom dots is 23" (58.5cm), so mark a dot 11.5" (29cm) to the left and another dot 11.5" (29cm) to the right of the center bottom dot. This is your bottom bell measure. Using the ruler, draw a light line connecting the top and bottom dots to make the sides of the bell, extending the line beyond the dots at both the top and bottom.

4. Along the extended side lines, measure 1" (2.5cm) beyond the dots on both the top and bottom and mark with a pencil. In step 8, this extra fabric will be folded inside the lampshade and hot-glued for a finished look. Our bell-shaped pieces were now 11" (28cm) high. Using a metal ruler and school chalk, horizontally connect the two very top dots with each other and the two very bottom dots with each other.

5. Repeat steps 3 and 4 to make a second bell-shaped piece of fabric.

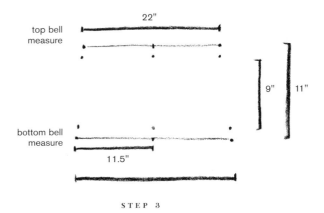

STEP 3

Assemble the Lampshade Cover

6. Cut the pieces out. With right sides facing, pin the pieces together along both sides. Machine-stitch the sides together with a ½" (13mm) seam allowance.

7. Heat up a glue gun. Meanwhile, press the seams open so that they lay flat. Turn the lampshade slipcover right side out and pull it over the shade, lining up one of the seams with the seam on the lampshade. The cover should fit snugly.

8. Cut slits in the fabric to accommodate the points where the exposed metal frame on the top of the shade meet the shade. Turn under ¼" (6mm) of the fabric to make a finished edge, then fold the remaining fabric over the rim of the shade, securing it with hot glue. Repeat on the bottom edge. Glue trim to the bottom edge if desired.

9. Place the lampshade on the lamp, positioning it so that neither seam is in the front.

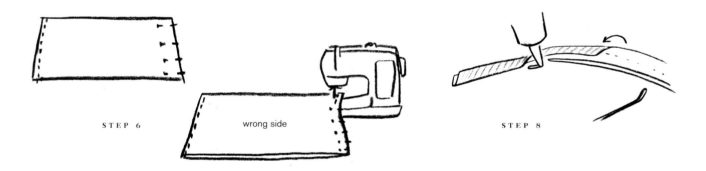

STEP 6   wrong side   STEP 8

<<< TRICK

If your lampshade has a really steep slope—it's more conical than cylindrical—you may have trouble gluing down your top fabric allowance, because it may not stretch enough to lie flat against the shade interior. Here's an easy fix: Cut a slit every few inches (4–8cm) in the excess fabric, then glue it section by section.

HOW TO REWIRE A LAMP

Now that you know how to customize a lampshade to fit into your decorating scheme, knowing how to rewire a lamp can serve you well. This is an especially useful skill if you are a frequent yard saler or flea marketer—how many times have you passed up a fabulous (but shadeless) lamp because it didn't work? There's really nothing to rewiring a lamp once you diagnose the reason it refuses to turn on. But if you find this brand of DIY daunting, or if for safety reasons a rewiring project seems better suited to a professional, by all means, consult an electrician.

First, see that the cord and plug are intact. If the cord is damaged, disconnect the plug from the electrical supply and cut the cord anywhere between the plug and the base of the lamp. You should see two insulated wires joined by the middle of the cord. Using a box cutter, split a new cord down the middle about 1½" (3.8cm), and then use a wire stripper to strip ½" (13mm) of insulation from each wire. Do the same on the cut end of the old cord. Next, using a Western Union splice, twist the old and new wires together. Cover the joined area with electrical tape.

If the cord is intact, test the socket. Unplug the lamp and unscrew the lightbulb. Squeeze the socket shell where it says PRESS and lift off the socket. Remove the cardboard insulating sleeve, unscrew the terminal screws, and disconnect the wires. Then use a continuity tester to test the socket. Attach it to the metal part of the body and place the probe on the silver terminal screw. If the tester lights up, the socket is fine—the problem may be the switch. Attach the tester's clip to the brass terminal screw, flip the lamp switch on, and place the probe on the round tab inside the socket. The tester will light if the socket and switch are good. If either is bad, purchase a new socket similar to the old one.

You can rewire an old working socket to a new cord or wire a new socket by wrapping the wire from the half of the cord covered with ridged insulation (this is the neutral wire) clockwise around the silver terminal screw and tighten. Wrap the other wire (from the smooth half of the cord) clockwise around the brass terminal and tighten. Test the connections, set the socket into place on the lamp, and return the sleeve and shell to their positions. Plug the lamp in and give yourself a pat on the back.

Western Union splice

EMBELLISHED *table* RUNNER

IF YOU CAN MEASURE AND CUT, then you can make this simple rectangular piece, the minimalist's version of a tablecloth. If you're new to machine-sewing, this is an excellent first project—it requires only very basic skills. For the more advanced sewer, it's a snap to make in just a few hours before a dinner party.

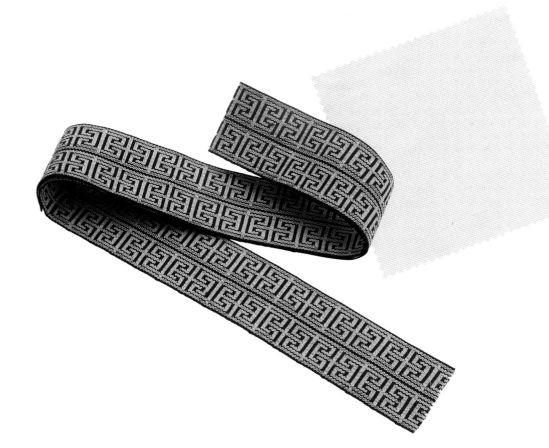

MATTHEW HALY'S BOOK OF UPHOLSTERY

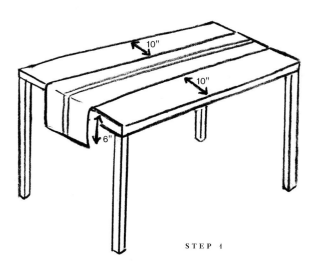

STEP 1

Measure and Cut the Fabric

1. Measure the width and length of your table. For a dining room table, the runner should leave at least 10" (25.5cm) of the table exposed on both sides and hang over the table by 6" (15cm) on each end. To calculate the dimensions of your runner, subtract 20" (51cm) from the width of the table and add 12" (30.5cm) to the length.

2. Lay the runner top fabric right side up on a work surface. Using a metal yardstick and school chalk, mark a rectangle on the fabric in the dimensions of your finished runner, adding ½" (13mm) on every side for the seam allowances. Our rectangle was 21" x 97" (53.5cm x 246cm).

3. Measure, mark, and cut a second rectangle in the same dimensions from the lining fabric for the underside of the runner. Set aside.

Place the Trim on the Runner

4. Lay the top of the runner right side up on a work surface (any surface into which pins can be inserted) and pull it taut, securing each of the 4 corners with pushpins. Measure the width of your trim. Ours was 2" (5cm) wide.

5. Using a metal yardstick and school chalk, mark the center of each short side of the runner top. Make another mark on each side of the center marks, half the width of the trim away from the center mark. Since our trim was 2" (5cm) wide, we marked 1" (2.5cm) from the center on each side. Connect the marks on each side of the center mark with the corresponding mark on the opposite end of the runner, using the yardstick as a guide.

MEASURING TABLE RUNNERS

There are no rules when it comes to determining how long a runner should be, but for rectangular tables, my decorator clients generally specify a 6–12" (15–30.5cm) overhang on each end. For round tables, I like the runner to stretch across the tabletop only—the table's curves would make an overhang lay awkwardly.

There are also no rules when it comes to the width of the runner, but there are considerations to take into account. When table runners first began to appear centuries ago as marks of wealth, they were woven on looms that were only so wide, but if you're sewing a runner from fabric, of course, you can make it as narrow or as wide as you like. Perhaps a helpful rule of thumb is to make the runner only as wide as will leave the table clear for large dinner plates on either side. That said, you can get creative with table runners by placing several in parallel across the width of the table, which lets them also serve as placemats.

Dining tables aren't the only places to consider putting runners, which are a great way to add color or pattern to any room when placed on end tables or nightstands. What's more, they can hide unsightly marks, scratches, or dents on secondhand tables.

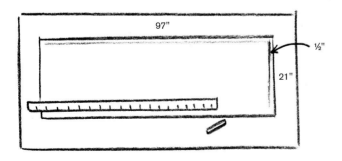

STEP 2

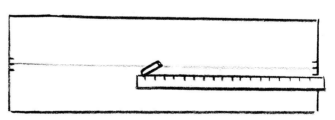

STEP 5

6. Pin the wrong side of the trim to the right side of the fabric, aligning each edge of the trim with the chalk lines. Using a sewing machine, topstitch the trim to the fabric using thread in a complementary or matching color (see Sewing Terms and Tools, page 180).

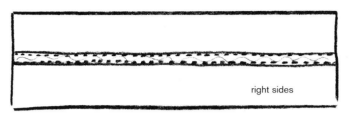

right sides

STEP 6

Assemble the Runner

7. With right sides together, pin the runner top to the lining. Beginning one-third of the way along the edge of one short side, machine-stitch the pieces together with a ½" (13mm) seam allowance. Stitch all the way around, leaving a 5–6" (13–15cm) opening on the short side where you began sewing. Trim the corners at an angle.

8. Turn the runner right side out. Pick at the corners with the sharp end of a needle, pulling the fabric out a little with each pick until each corner is perfectly square.

9. Press the runner with an iron, pressing the seams out by kneading them with your fingers as you go. Press the opening so that the seam allowance is tucked inside the runner.

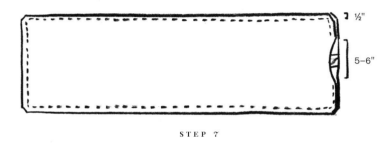

½"

5–6"

STEP 7

Finishing

10. To finish, topstitch along the inside edge of the runner, as close to the edge as possible, using thread in a matching or complementary color.

STEP 8

LINED *round* TABLECLOTH

KNOWLEDGE OF SIMPLE MACHINE-STITCHING is all you need to make this elegant tablecloth. Once you learn the formula for how much fabric you need, you can make a cover for a round table of any size. It's all about the measuring and cutting, so take the time to get it right. Choose washable fabric and wash it before stitching the tablecloth together—you don't want a floor-length tablecloth to shrink even ½" (13mm). I made this one for a dining room table with a total measurement of 96" (244cm) from the floor to the tabletop, across the table, and down to the floor again. Most upholstery fabrics are 54–56" (137–142cm) wide, which necessitates stitching several widths together (unless your tablecloth is for a smaller side

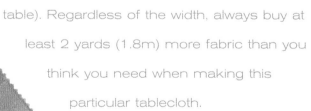

table). Regardless of the width, always buy at least 2 yards (1.8m) more fabric than you think you need when making this particular tablecloth.

NOTE | **How to Make an Unlined Tablecloth**

Add another ½" (13mm) to the length and width of the main measurement to determine the exact amount of fabric needed. Add about 20" (50cm) to this number as in step 2. Skip step 6. To stitch a finished hem, place the tablecloth on a work surface with the right side facing you. Fold the edge under ½" (13mm), press, and fold under again ½" (13mm), pinning through all thicknesses as you make your way around the entire tablecloth. With the right side facing you, machine-stitch the hem in place.

Measure and Cut the Fabric

1. To determine how much fabric you'll need, measure the diameter of the table. The table pictured is 36" (92cm) across. Measure the height of the table, double it, and add this number to the diameter. Then add 1" (2.5cm) to both the height and width for two ½" (13mm) seam allowances. Our main length totaled 97" (246cm).

Double this number to obtain the total length of fabric to buy: We needed a 97" (246cm) wide tablecloth, so with the 97" (246cm) of length also needed, we needed a total of 194" (492cm), or 5.3 yd (4.8m). Add at least 20" (50cm) to that total. For our tablecloth, I started with 6 yd (5.5m) to give myself a margin.

2. Cut 2 pieces from the full width of the fabric, each 10" (25cm) longer than the main length from step 1 (since we needed 97" [246cm] of length, we cut two 107" [271cm] pieces). The extra 10" (25cm) of fabric allows it to pull in a bit when seamed together and folded. Fold one piece of the fabric in half lengthwise with the selvedge edges together, press, and cut along the fold.

3. With right sides together, pin the selvedge edges of the halved panels to the selvedge edges of the larger panel. Machine-stitch together with a ½" (13mm) seam allowance. Press the seams open. Our sewn panel was 107" x 108" (271cm x 274cm), including the selvedges.

4. Fold the piece in half crosswise then lengthwise, lining up the edges and sliding a metal yardstick between the folds to make them crisp and to smooth the fabric so that it lays flat. If the edges are not precisely aligned and there are puckers in the folds, your tablecloth will have a roughly scalloped, uneven edge.

5. Place the folded fabric on a work surface with the single-fold edge on your right and the cut edges at the top and left.

Grasp the full thickness of fabric in the bottom left corner and bring that corner to the fold at your right to form a triangle. Rotate the fabric clockwise 90 degrees so that the right angle of the triangle is on your right. Then determine the length of the tablecloth from the center of the table to the floor by splitting the main length from step 1 in half (we divided 97" [246cm] by 2, giving us 48½" [123cm]). Mark the fabric at that distance from the bottom left point to the top point. Using a metal tape measure and school chalk, measure and mark the same length (48½" [123cm] for our tablecloth) from the bottom left point at several points fanning out along the entire triangle. Lock the metal tape measure at this length to ensure consistent measures. Connect the points with the school chalk to create an arc. Cut through all thicknesses of fabric along the arc, making sure to keep the fabric smoothly folded.

6. The lining will be the same size as the fabric. Because it doesn't matter if there's a seam down the middle of the lining, you needn't cut one panel in half (step 2). Cut two 107" [271cm] pieces from the full width of the lining fabric. With right sides and selvedges together, pin and machine-stitch the 2 lining pieces together, starting at one end and stopping one-third of the length across. Repeat on the other end, again stopping one-third of the distance across. (After stitching the lining and fabric together, you will use the opening to turn the tablecloth right side out.) Press seam open. Place the main fabric on top of the lining, trace the shape to be cut, and cut out the lining.

Assemble the Tablecloth

7. With the right sides of the lining and tablecloth together and the edges aligned, pin the two pieces together. Machine-stitch with ½" (13mm) seam allowance. Turn the tablecloth right side out, knead out the seams with your fingers, and press. Hand-stitch the lining seam closed.

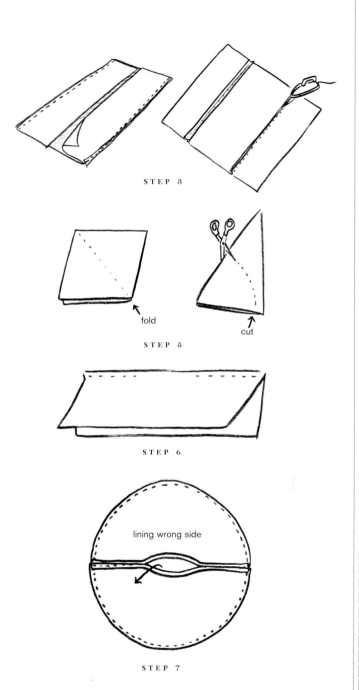

STEP 3

fold   cut

STEP 5

STEP 6

lining wrong side

STEP 7

BASIC *throw* PILLOW

THE SECRET TO MAKING PILLOWS that are comfortably taut—
no slack in the fabric and no pressure on the seams—is twofold.
First, use a template bowed out on each side by about ¾" (19mm)
to make the pillow look like it has four straight sides. The other key is
to use an insert that is 2" (5cm) larger than the pillow's dimensions.
The following projects use this basic throw pillow pattern, with added
instructions on making them in different sizes and using various trims.

MATERIALS

- ¾ yd (68.5cm) upholstery fabric

- ¾ yd (68.5cm) muslin, to make a pattern (optional)

- School chalk

- Flexible yardstick

- Dressmaker's pins

- Machine-stitching thread in a complementary color

- Medium-weight zipper in a color complementary to the fabric, 1" (2.5cm) shorter than the length of the bowed side

- 18" (45.5cm) square pillow insert of desired firmness

FINISHED MEASUREMENTS

All materials are for a 16" (40.5cm) square basic throw pillow. Adjust according to the size desired.

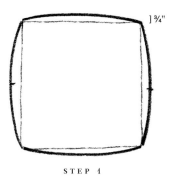

1¾"

STEP 1

NOTE | **What Size Insert Do I need?**

Using an insert that is larger than the finished measurement of the pillow is standard practice; the extra inches ensure that the pillow won't appear deflated and that the cover is taut. If you prefer a looser look, by all means experiment with other sizes to find a fit you like. The inserts used here are 2" (5cm) larger than the finished measurement of the pillow, but the larger the pillow, the more you need to add to the size of the insert. For example, an 18" (46cm) square pillow takes a 20" (51cm) square insert, whereas a 24" (61cm) pillow looks better with a 27" (69cm) square insert.

Make a Template

1. If you're going to make several pillows, make a muslin pattern first (if you're making a single pillow, you can perform this step directly on the upholstery fabric, skip step 2, and trace the pillow front to make the back). Add ½" (13mm) for the seam allowance to the finished measurement of each side. Measure and mark your square on the muslin (our pillow was 16" (40.5cm) square, so we marked a 17" (43cm) square to include seam allowances). Mark the halfway point on each side of the square with school chalk. Using a flexible yardstick and chalk, measure and mark ¾" (19mm) beyond the mark on each side. Using the side of the yardstick, create an arc joining one corner, the middle mark, and the opposite corner for each side. Mark the fabric along the curved edge of the yardstick to indicate the bowed

sides. Cut out the pattern along the marked curves, fold it in half, and trim so that the raw edges line up.

Cut and Prep the Fabric

2. Place the muslin pattern on the fabric, right side up. If the fabric is patterned, position the muslin so that the design motifs appear on the pillow as desired. Trace around the muslin onto the fabric with school chalk. Repeat to make a second panel and cut out both.

3. Fold each panel in half crosswise so that the sides meet. Notch at both ends of the fold on each panel.

Insert the Zipper

4. With the right sides of the pillow panels together, the front and back notches aligned, and beginning at one of the back corners, machine-stitch along the back edge to 2" (5cm) from the corner. Flip the whole thing over and machine-stitch 2" (5cm) along the opposite side of the back edge (A). Turn the pillow right side out. Fold under the remaining back edge of both panels ½" (13mm) (B).

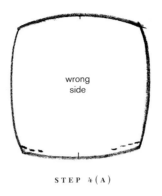

wrong side

STEP 4 (A)

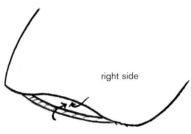

right side

STEP 4 (B)

STEP 4 (C)

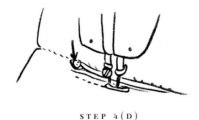

STEP 4 (D)

NOTE | **Inserting Zippers**

For the projects in this book requiring zippers, make sure the zipper is cut about 2" (5cm) longer than the opening into which it is being inserted, so that the backstitch at the beginning and ending of the stitch is made over the zipper ends. This prevents the zipper slide from slipping out of the finished project.

With the zipper closed, center it from the inside of the panels along one of the folded edges so that the fold meets the center of the zipper's teeth. Pin (C). Using a zipper foot, machine-stitch one side of the zipper to the panel, positioning the needle as close to the teeth as possible and butting the zipper foot up against the teeth (D). Stitch to just inside the 2" (5cm) seam on the opposite end, then stitch over the teeth to the other side. Stitch the remaining side of the zipper to the folded edge, opening the zipper as you go. Backstitch beyond the zipper on both ends.

Assemble the Pillow

5. With right sides together, line up the front notches on the two panels of fabric and pin the three remaining sides together. Beginning at a back corner, machine-stitch all the way around.

6. Turn the pillow right side out and fill with the desired insert (see Fill 'Er Up, right), smoothing it so that the pillow is uniformly taut.

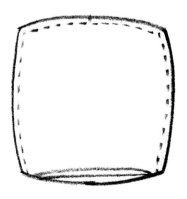

STEP 5

NOTE | Fill 'Er Up

There are several insert options available for pillows—choose one based on the degree of softness you want and the amount of money you are willing to spend.

- The most luxurious pillow is an 80/20 percent mix of down and feathers. It is the softest and most requested by upscale decorators. Choose it if the pillows are going to be used often, say, to prop up your head on a sofa or bed.
- A mix of 60/40 down and feathers is slightly firmer and less expensive than the softer mix. I find it perfectly comfortable and perhaps the smartest choice if your budget is not unlimited.
- Synthetic Dacron forms are the least expensive option. They're best used for pillows that are purely decorative, since the filler doesn't provide much in the way of comfort.

If you are going to use an 80/20 or 60/40 insert, avoid using heavy upholstery or stiff fabric, which will blunt the feather-light feeling of the filling.

THROW *pillow* WITH BOX TRIM

THE METHOD FOR MAKING ANY PILLOW with a flat trim, such as the
"pleated" fringe here, is essentially the same as making a basic throw
pillow, but with the added step of stitching trim to the top panel. I used
toile for this pillow and wanted to center one of the fabric's larger scenes
on the front and back of the pillow, so I needed a little extra fabric. The
amount of patterned fabric you'll need depends on the size of the pattern
repeat. Keep this in mind when you're purchasing fabric—it doesn't hurt
to bring your project instructions with you to guarantee you're getting
enough to incorporate the design you want.

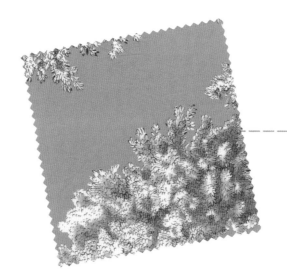

Make a Template and Cut and Prep the Fabric

1. Follow the steps for making a basic pillow (Basic Throw Pillow, page 36) through step 3. For the pillow shown here, the muslin square was 19" (23cm).

Add the Trim

2. Pin the trim along the edge of the right side of the top panel, lining up the raw edges and beginning with the cut end of the trim at the back notch. Machine-stitch the trim to the fabric with a ½" (13mm) seam allowance. As you approach a corner, stitch to within ½" (13mm) of it, leaving the needle down. Raise the presser foot, pivot the fabric around the needle, and sew along the next side. As you approach the end, cut one end of the trim so that it overlaps slightly with the other. Fold the overlap under and stitch the last bit of trim to the pillow.

Assemble the Pillow

3. Follow steps 4 through 6 for making a basic pillow (Basic Throw Pillow, page 36).

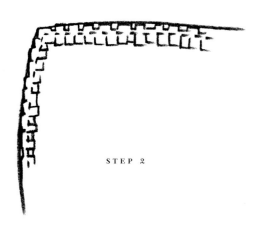

STEP 2

THROW *pillow* WITH WELTING

WELTING IS FABRIC-COVERED CORD sewn into the seam between two adjoining pieces of fabric, as in the case of this pillow. Welting is often referred to as cording or piping, but it is distinct from decorative cording that is hot-glued or hand-stitched to upholstery to emphasize edges. I use ready-made welting here, which is a good option for a first foray into sewing and upholstery. What's more, it saves a bit of time. On the other hand, making your own welting allows for unlimited options—you can make it out of almost any fabric you like (see the Sew Your Own Welting box on page 49).

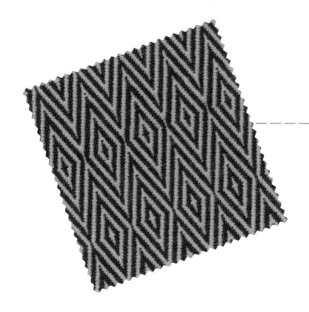

MATERIALS

- 1–1¼ yd (114cm) upholstery fabric
- 1–1¼ yd (114cm) muslin, to make a pattern (optional)
- School chalk
- Flexible yardstick
- Dressmaker's pins
- Machine-stitching thread in a complementary color
- 2½ yd (2.3m) jute welting
- 19" (48cm) long medium-weight zipper in a color complementary to the fabric
- 22" (56cm) square pillow insert of desired firmness

FINISHED MEASUREMENTS

All materials are for a 20" (51cm) square pillow. Adjust according to the size you desire.

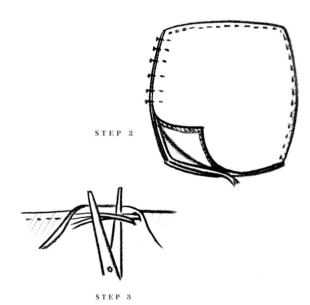

STEP 2

STEP 3

Make a Template and Cut and Prep the Fabric

1. Follow the steps for making a basic pillow through step 3 (Basic Throw Pillow, page 36). For the pillow shown here, each side of the square marked on the muslin was 21" (53cm).

Add the Welting

2. Pin the welting along the edges of the right side of the top panel, lining up the raw edges and positioning the cut ends at the back notch. There should be excess welting where it meets at the back notch. Machine-stitch the welting to the top panel with a ½" (13mm) seam allowance, beginning at the back notch and working around the entire panel. As you approach a corner, stitch to within ½" (13mm) of it, leaving the needle down. Cut into the fabric to within ⅛" (3mm) of the stitching line, placing your scissors at an angle to the machine needle. Raise the presser foot, pivot the fabric, and sew along the next side.

3. To join the ends of the jute welting, cut open 4" (10cm) of the welting at each end using a seam ripper. Lay the jute out flat with one piece overlapping the other. Being careful not to cut the jute fabric, trim the cords on an angle so that they meet. Fold down one jute strip over the cord. Fold the cut edge of the other jute strip under 1" (2.5cm), then fold it over the cord so that it lays flat on the other end of the cord's fabric. Stitch to the fabric panel.

Assemble the Pillow

4. Follow steps 4 through 6 for making a basic pillow (Basic Throw Pillow, page 36).

SEW YOUR OWN WELTING

Why make your own welting? Indeed, there are hundreds of premade styles to choose from, but if you want welting to exactly match the fabric of your pillow, then making it is the only way to go. The key to making professional-looking welting is to stitch the cord into the fabric as tightly as possible. If you don't already have a welting foot for your sewing machine, I strongly suggest you buy one. The standard sewing foot doesn't allow you to get close enough to the cording to stitch it snugly into the fabric. Stick to fabrics of average thickness for the best results: Leather and thick weaves are generally tough to stitch on a home sewing machine.

1. Cut 1½" (3.8cm) wide strips of fabric on the bias or crosswise grain. Cut the short ends on a 45-degree angle.

2. Align the short ends, right sides together, so that the ends form a V shape. Pin. Machine-stitch the strips together with a ½" (13mm) seam allowance along the short edge. Press the seams open.

3. Fold the strips lengthwise over the cording, aligning raw edges. Machine-stitch the cord into the fabric with the needle as close to the cord as possible.

4. Follow the project instructions for stitching the welting into your piece.

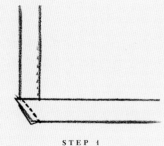

STEP 1

STEP 2

FABRIC TIP >>>

When using a woven fabric, it is not always readily apparent which side is the front and which is the back. Before cutting, mark the back side of these fabrics with school chalk to ensure that you are working on the correct side.

THROW *pillow* WITH A FLANGE

A FLANGE IS A BORDER OF FABRIC created by topstitching through both of the front and back fabric around the rim—as little as ½" (13mm) or as much as 2" (5cm) away from the edge. Here, I've topstitched just ½" (13mm) away from the edge, a technique that produces the effect of welting. Keep in mind that the size of the pillow is measured by the area within the flange. When making your pattern for this pillow, add ½" (13mm) to each side in addition to the ½" (13mm) on each side for the seam allowance.

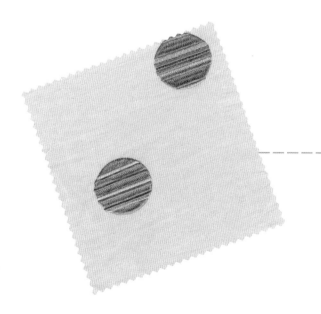

MATERIALS

- 1½ yd (1.4m) upholstery fabric
- 1½ yd (1.4m) muslin, to make a pattern (optional)
- School chalk
- Flexible yardstick
- Dressmaker's pins
- Machine-stitching thread in a complementary color
- 21" (53cm) long medium-weight zipper
- 24" (61cm) square pillow insert of desired firmness

FINISHED MEASUREMENTS

All materials are for a 22" (56cm) square pillow. Adjust according to the size you desire.

Make the Pillow

1. Follow the steps for making a basic pillow (Basic Throw Pillow, page 36) through step 5. For this pillow, each side of the square marked on the muslin was 24" (61cm).

Embellish the Pillow

2. Turn right side out, kneading out the seams with your fingers. Topstitch ½" (13mm) away from the edge around the perimeter of the cover, beginning at the back edge where the zipper ends and stitching all the way around to the other end. Fill with the desired insert (see Note on page 41), smoothing it so that the pillow is uniformly taut.

STEP 2

SADDLE-*stitched* BOLSTER

BOLSTERS CAN BE AS SIMPLE AS THIS ONE, with no bells and whistles, or quite flamboyant, with ruches, buttons, and tassels. I advise my students to master the basic bolster first and then move on to more elaborate versions.

There are several different fillings appropriate for bolsters. Foam is the firmest option, a good choice for a bolster meant as a lumbar pillow to help support the back. Other options include a semi-firm mixture of foam chips and down, or the very softest filling, down and feathers. Note that down and feathers can actually be too soft, especially if you want the bolster to maintain its crisp, cylindrical shape.

Because sewing in a circle tends to be more difficult, avoid using slippery fabrics such as silks, which pucker easily. I like to make this bolster in leather, in fact, because the saddle stitching looks quite handsome. Use leather only if your machine is a workhorse, however.

- 1 yd (91cm) fabric

- Large protractor or plate with a diameter 1" (2.5cm) larger than that of the bolster (see step 1)

- 14" (35.5cm) medium-weight zipper in a complementary color

- Dressmaker's pins

- Machine-stitching thread in a color contrasting the bolster fabric

- 8" (20.5cm) diameter x 18"(46cm) long insert of desired firmness (see tip, below)

FINISHED MEASUREMENTS

- All materials are for an 8" (20cm) diameter x 18" (46cm) long bolster. The circumference of the pillow is approximately 25" (63.5cm). Adjust according to the size you desire.

Cut the Fabric

1. Mark and cut two 9" (23cm) diameter disks from the fabric (the diameter of the finished bolster, 8" [20.5cm], plus two ½" [13mm] seam allowances), using a protractor and school chalk or tracing a 9" (23cm) plate with the chalk. Mark and cut a 19" x 26" (48cm x 66cm) rectangle (the length of the finished bolster, 18" [46cm], plus two ½" seam allowances, by the circumference of the bolster, 25" [63.5cm], plus ½" [13mm] on each end for attaching the zipper). If you are working with patterned fabric, mark to center the desired design motif on both the disks and the rectangle.

2. Fold the disks in half, and notch on both ends of the fold. Fold the rectangle in half lengthwise, and notch on both ends of the fold.

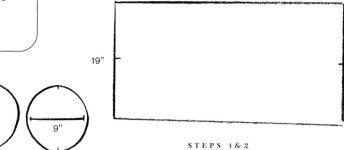

STEPS 1 & 2

<<< **MEASURING TIP**

Bolsters are always measured by the diameter of the circle and the length of the bolster. Standard foam fillers are available in 6" (15cm), 8" (20.5cm), 10" (25.5cm), and 12" (30.5cm) diameters, and must be wrapped in ½" (13mm) Dacron (see page 181).

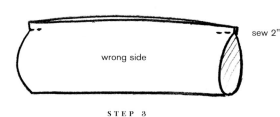

STEP 3

Sew the Pillow and Insert the Zipper

3. With right sides together, fold the rectangle in half, lining up the raw edges of the long sides. With a ½" (13mm) seam allowance, machine-stitch along the long sides just 2" (5cm) in from each end, leaving an opening for the zipper. Turn right side out.

4. Open the zipper fully. Fold under ½" (13mm) of the raw edge on one side of the opening. Pin one side of the zipper to the folded edge, positioning the fold on the center of the teeth. Using a zipper foot, machine-stitch as close to the teeth as possible, butting the zipper foot up against the teeth. Backstitch beyond the zipper on both ends. Close the zipper, fold under ½" (13mm) of the remaining raw edge, and pin the remaining side of the zipper to the fabric as for the first side and machine-stitch it in the same way.

5. Turn the body inside out. With right sides together, pin the disks to the bolster body, lining up the raw edges. Machine-stitch the discs to the body with a ½" (13mm) seam allowance. Cut notches in the seam allowance to ease the tension as you stitch around the curves, making sure not to cut into the seam. Repeat with the second disk on the other end of the bolster body.

6. Turn the bolster right side out and open the seams with your fingers. For the saddle stitch, topstitch on the body of the bolster around the circumference of the disks on each end and then around the perimeter of both disks, positioning the foot as close to the seam as possible (see page 195).

Finishing

7. Fill the bolster with the desired insert and zip closed.

TRICK OF THE TRADE >>>

How to do the math: To determine circumference, multiply the diameter by 3.14. Round to the nearest whole number.

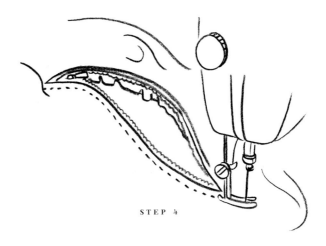

STEP 4

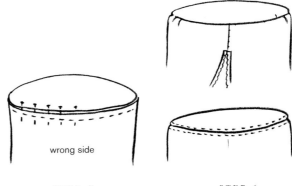

wrong side

STEP 5

STEP 6

DIRECTOR'S *chair*

THIS IS AMONG THE MOST STRAIGHTFORWARD of upholstery projects. You're essentially making two double-sided panels—one for the seat, the other for the back—by folding lengths of fabric and sewing the raw edges together. I prefer doubling up on the thickness of the fabric to give the back a finished look and make the seat less likely to stretch and sag over time.

Your director's chair may not be exactly the same style as this one, but the basic method of stretching fabric between wood rails is the same.

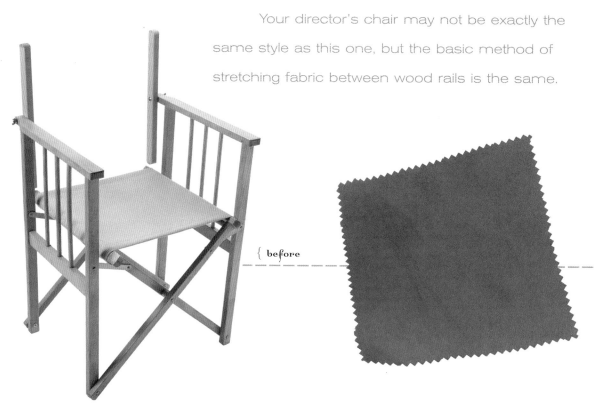

{ before

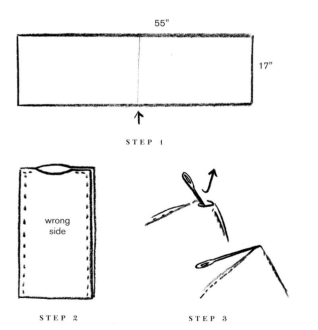

55"

17"

STEP 1

wrong
side

STEP 2   STEP 3

Measure and Cut the Fabric

1. Cut a length of fabric the width of the finished seat by twice the depth of the seat plus ½" (13mm) on each side for the seam allowances. Our seat piece measured 17" x 43" (43cm x 109cm). Cut a second length of fabric the width of the back by twice the height of the back, adding ½" (13mm) on each side for the seam allowances. Our back piece measured 17" x 55" (43cm x 140cm). Note: When measuring the width, remember to include the amount of fabric that wraps around the frame and attaches to it.

Sew the Seat and Back

2. With right sides together, fold the seat fabric in half crosswise, lining up the raw edges. Pin along the raw edges inside the ½" (13mm) seam allowance. Beginning near the fold, machine-stitch the raw edges together with a ½" (13mm) seam allowance. As you approach a corner, stitch to within ½" (13mm) of it; leaving the needle down, raise the presser foot and pivot the fabric 90 degrees, and then sew one-third of the short side (opposite the fold). Flip the seat over and machine-stitch the remaining raw edges together, leaving an opening on the short side through which you will turn the piece.

3. Turn the seat right side out. Using the sharp end of a sewing needle, pick at the corners, pulling the fabric out a little with each pick to make them perfectly square. Knead out the seams with your hands by rubbing them between your thumb and fingers.

4. Fold under ½" (13mm) of the raw edges of the short side's opening and pin. Topstitch along the finished edges as close to the seam line as possible, beginning on the short side and stitching all the way around the pieces, sewing the opening on the short side closed. Note: If you also want to add decorative topstitching on this chair, like I did, use a metal yardstick and school chalk to measure and mark the desired distance from the edge of the fabric. Here, I measured and marked the seat and back 2" (5cm) from the edge. Topstitch on the line.

5. Repeat steps 2–4 for the seat back.

Attach the Seat and Back to the Frame

6. Replace the seat and back on the chair, using the old upholstery as your guide and making sure the pile of the fabric is going in the right direction (see the Fabric Tip, below right). Use a regulator or awl to poke a hole through the fabric if necessary to attach it to the rails. Staple the seat and back to the frame, using the old staple marks as your guide.

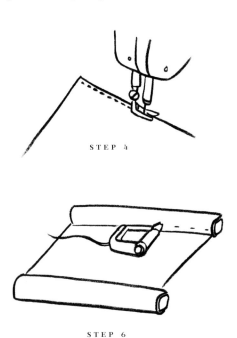

STEP 4

STEP 6

FABRIC TIP >>>

When using fabrics with a pile, or brush, take care to cut the fabric so that it goes in the right direction. To determine the direction of the pile, brush the fabric with your fingers. If it is smooth, you're brushing with the pile; if it's rough, you're brushing against the pile. For all upholstered sofas and chairs, there's an easy rule of thumb for cutting pile fabrics: The pile should be smooth when you brush it down on all vertical surfaces, and forward, from the back of the chair to the front, on all horizontal surfaces. The one exception is a rolled arm; in this case the pile should be smooth when you brush toward the seat.

intermediate

THE PROJECTS

Consider this chapter an introduction to upholstery tools, techniques, and materials. Through the projects included here, you will become adept at using an electric staple gun and tacking hammer while honing such techniques as making a rolled edge on a cushion, smoothing fabric over a curved edge, and using the Four-Point Tacking and Stapling Technique. An upholsterer's material stock-in-trade shows up here, too: Foam, Dacron, tacking strip, buckram, tacks and decorative nails, and various adhesives are required to cover this chapter's trio of stools.

All of the pieces I've chosen for this chapter are small scale. And for good reason: Upholstery fabric is expensive, perhaps the most expensive part of the upholstery equation, and working with a little bit of it is just like working with a lot. Why not practice your skills on the Fringed Cube-Shaped Pouf (page 112) or the Boudoir Stool (page 118) before embarking on anything larger and hence more expensive? Once you are comfortable with such endeavors

as shooting staples with an electric staple gun and pinching the edge of a foam cushion just so to round it, then by all means, bring on the long benches and full-scale ottomans. The techniques for upholstering them are exactly the same as those described in this chapter—you'll just need to spend more money on the fabric and supplies to do it.

As you already know, measuring plays a primary role in the world of upholstery. Nowhere is this more true than in the world of windows. I've included soft goods such as a Roman shade, floor-length drapes, and a slipcover in this chapter not because they are necessarily more difficult to sew than those projects in the earlier chapter, but because getting the precise measurements down is somewhat more challenging. You should have experience with measuring and cutting before embarking on dressing up your windows—the results of the practiced student are always far superior to those of a beginner. Not only that, but the earned gratification becomes a bit addicting; you'll want to upholster everything in the house!

bench WITH DECORATIVE NAILS

THIS UPHOLSTERED PIECE has a relaxed fit, which I achieved by refraining from pulling the fabric too tight while stapling it to the frame. Though it is somewhat looser than, say, the Leather Bureau Chair on page 162, it still looks crisp because the tension of the fabric is uniform across the stool. Two pieces of foam make up the layers of the cushion—a thin piece is glued under firmer, thicker foam, creating a crown.

Decorative upholstery nails give the piece handsome detail, but they must be level, evenly spaced, and in straight lines for the proper effect. The eye is immediately drawn to them, so a beautiful piece can look sloppy if the nails aren't just so. And though not essential, they do give the piece a bit more cachet.

{ before

- 5 yd (4.6m) jute webbing
- 1 yd (91cm) heavy-duty burlap
- 8" x 16" (20.5cm x 40.5cm) piece of ¼" (6mm) foam
- Electric kitchen knife or hacksaw blade
- 313 adhesive spray
- 10" x 18" (25cm x 46cm) of 1½" (3.8cm) LX45 blue foam
- 74 adhesive spray
- ¾ yd (68.5cm) ½" (13mm) Dacron
- 1 yd (91cm) upholstery fabric
- Box cutter or razor blade
- 2 yd (1.8m) complementary trim
- Nylon-tipped tacking hammer
- Approximately sixty ½" (13mm) #9 nickel nails
- 1 yd (91cm) cambric
- Basic upholstery tools (See page 15)

FINISHED MEASUREMENTS

- All materials are for a 12" x 20" (30.5cm x 51cm) box seat. Adjust according to the size of your seat.

Prepare the Frame

1. Strip the stool down to its frame (see Stripping Furniture, page 188).

2. Staple the jute webbing to the frame (see Attaching Webbing to a Frame, page 190).

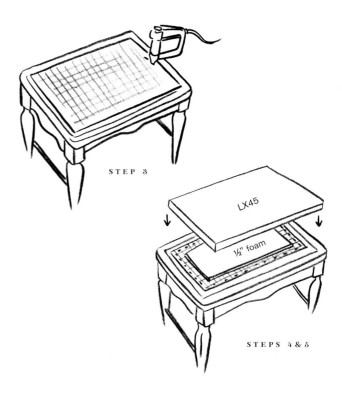

STEP 3

STEPS 4 & 5

<<< FABRIC TIP

If you are working with a patterned fabric and want to center a particular design on the seat, mark the center of the design with school chalk on the right side of the fabric. Divide the depth and width of the measure for the cut fabric in half. Our halved measurements are 8" (20cm) for the depth and 14" (35.5cm) for the width. Using a metal yardstick, mark the fabric at these measurements from the center chalk mark.

3. Lay the burlap over the webbing and trim the short sides to within ¼" (6mm) of the edges of the frame. Using the Four-Point Tacking and Stapling Technique (page 189), staple the burlap to the frame just beyond the edge of the webbing. Fold the burlap onto itself and repeat the four-point tacking and stapling technique.

Prepare the Padding

4. Cut a piece of the ¼" (6mm) foam to measure 2" (5cm) less on all sides than the finished box seat (see Cutting Foam, page 192). Spray one side of the foam all over with the 313 adhesive. Spray the burlap with the 313 adhesive, covering only the area where the foam will be affixed. Wait about 2 minutes for the adhesive to become tacky, then center the ¼" (6mm) foam, glue side down, on the burlap. Press down on it all over with your hands to affix.

5. Cut the LX45 blue foam to the dimensions of the affixed burlap. Spray one side of the foam and all edges with

74 adhesive. Spray the top of the ¼" (6mm) foam and the rim of burlap all over with the 74 adhesive. Wait about 3–5 minutes for the adhesive to become tacky, then center the blue foam glue side down onto the ¼" (6mm) foam and burlap. Press down on it all over with your hands to affix.

6. Roll the edges of the blue foam (see Making a Rolled Edge, page 193).

7. Drape the piece of ½" (13mm) Dacron over the foam and, working as close to the foam as possible, staple it to the frame using the Four-Point Stapling Technique (page 189). Note: While stapling these layers, leave space for the fabric and the decorative nails. If you staple every layer close to the finished wood, then the nails will sit too high when they're inserted. Trim the excess Dacron.

Measure and Cut the Fabric

8. To determine how much upholstery fabric you need, measure the length and width of the cushion with a dressmaker's measuring tape. Ours measured 12" x 24" (30.5cm x 61cm). Add 2" (5cm) to each side and cut out a piece of fabric in these dimensions. Our piece of fabric measured 16" x 28" (40.5cm x 71cm).

Attach the Fabric to the Stool

9. Measure and mark the center of your stool seat and the center of your fabric with an X. Place your fabric on your piece, lining up the Xs. Pin the fabric to the Dacron in the center using 2 upholstery pins.

10. Using the tacking hammer and upholstery tacks, "pin" the fabric in place temporarily using the Four-Point Tacking and Stapling Technique (page 189), smoothing the fabric and keeping the tension consistent as you work. Space the tacks about 2" (5cm) apart and do not hammer them in too far.

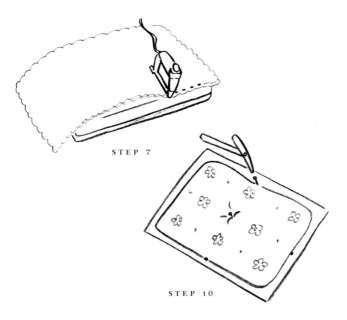

STEP 7

STEP 10

11. Staple the fabric to the frame, beginning in the middle of a long side and working your way around the cushion. Position your staple gun as close to the cushion as possible and space the staples about ⅛" (3mm) apart. Since the tacks have not been hammered in too far—they were inserted only to tack the fabric in place—you should be able to knock them out with the side of your staple gun as you move along the frame. If they have been inserted deeply, use pincers to remove them.

12. Using a razor, cut away excess fabric as close to the staples as possible.

Attach the Trim

13. Heat up the glue gun. Put a dab of hot glue on the cut end of the trim and fold it back onto itself to create a finished edge and prevent it from unraveling. Beginning in a corner, apply hot glue to the short side of the seat along the edge of the fabric. Affix the trim along this side, making sure it is straight as you apply pressure to it with your fingers. When you reach a corner, fold the trim back and staple the fold to the frame at a 45-degree angle to the corner. Then fold the trim back over the staple to cover it, and continue gluing the trim onto the next side. To finish, turn the raw edge of the trim under and hot glue it to the frame.

14. Using a metal yardstick and a pencil, mark the trim every 1" (2.5cm) or in other equal increments depending on desired spacing of the upholstery nails. (Use fewer nails for a fabric with a busy pattern.) Using a nylon-tipped tacking hammer to protect the decorative nails, hammer the nails into the trim at each pencil mark.

15. Place the stool upside down on a work surface. Drape a piece of cambric over the exposed webbing and trim to the dimensions of the interior of the frame plus 1" (2.5cm) on each side. Turn the raw edges under 1" (2.5cm) and tack to the frame with upholstery nails using the Four-Point Tacking Technique (page 189).

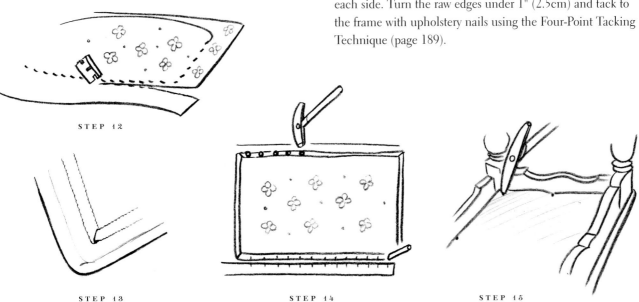

STEP 12

STEP 13

STEP 14

STEP 15

CUSTOM-*built* CORNICE

IF YOU'RE LOOKING for a way to turn a post-college place into a space that's a bit more grown up and sophisticated, installing cornices over your windows isn't a bad place to begin. They can turn average windows into very tailored, smart-looking ones without investing too much time or money in your window treatments. They can be the sole decorative element on a window or one of several. Most of my clients combine them with curtains and sometimes Roman shades. Their styles vary widely—some clients prefer the same fabric for the cornice and drapes, while others choose complementary fabrics. Here I combined a neutral drape with an upholstered cornice in a patterned fabric, a nice combination if you want to inject a room with a bit of pattern but don't want to cover the entire window in it. It's also an inexpensive way to use a fabric that might be too pricey for full-length curtains.

This project can use an existing cornice, but instructions are also included for building a new one.

MATERIALS

- 313 adhesive
- 1 yd (91cm) ½" (13mm) Dacron
- 1 yd (91cm) upholstery fabric
- 1½ yd (1.4m) drapery lining
- Two 2" (5cm) L brackets
- Four 2" (5cm) #6 wood screws
- Basic upholstery tools (See page 15)

MATERIALS FOR BUILDING YOUR OWN CORNICE

- 50" x 12" (127cm x 30.5cm) piece ½" (13mm) plywood for the face
- Two 12" x 4½" (30.5cm x 11cm) pieces ½" (13mm) plywood for the sides
- 50" x 5" (126cm x 11cm) piece ½" (13mm) plywood for the top
- Wood glue
- Eight 1" (2.5cm) #6 wood screws

FINISHED MEASUREMENTS

- All materials are for a 50" (127cm) wide x 5" (13cm) deep x 12" (5cm) high cornice. Adjust according to the size you desire.

Prepare the Frame

1. If you are using an existing cornice, strip it down to the frame (see Stripping Furniture, page 188).

2. If you are making a new cornice, make it 4" (10cm) wider on both sides than the width of the window from the outside edges of the molding. Our window was 42" (107cm) wide from molding edge to molding edge, so we made our cornice 50" (127cm) wide. Glue and screw (with #6 wood screws) the face and returns (sides) of the cornice together, lining up the edges of the returns along the inside edge of the face. Insert the top of the cornice in place and glue and screw it to the face and returns. Let the glue dry for about 1 hour.

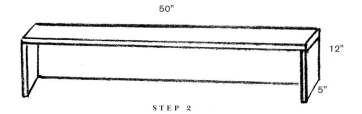

50"

12"

5"

STEP 2

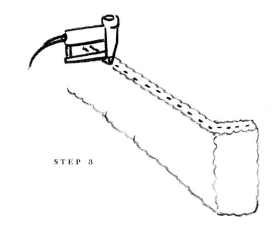

STEP 3

3. Spray the front and returns of the frame with the 313 adhesive. Wait 2 minutes until tacky, and wrap the front and returns of the frame in the Dacron, stapling it to the narrow edge along the back of the cornice. Trim away the excess. Using a permanent marker, measure and mark the middle of the front of the cornice at the top and bottom edges. Set aside.

Measure and Cut the Fabric

4. To determine the dimensions of the piece of fabric to cut, measure the cornice with the Dacron from the back edge of one side and across the front to the back edge of the other side, including the back edges in the measurement. Add 6" (15cm) to the measurement (2" [5cm] for wrapping each side plus four ½" [13mm] seam allowances). To determine the depth, measure the padded cornice from the bottom inside edge up the height of the cornice and to the top edge, adding 4" (5cm) to wrap it over the top and under the bottom. The dimensions of the fabric needed to cover our cornice were 66" (168cm) wide x 16" (40.5cm) high.

5. The fabric you use will likely not be wide enough to cut a single strip that adds up to the width and depth of the cornice; here, I cut two strips of fabric and, to avoid having a seam in the front of the cornice, cut one strip in half and stitched the three pieces together.

Cut two 16" (41cm) long strips of fabric across the roll. Fold one of the strips in half crosswise and cut along the fold. These two pieces (7½" [9cm] long) will cover the sides of the cornice; the longer piece (51" [129.5] long) will cover the front, and your seams will lie at the corners. With right sides together, machine-stitch the sides to the front along the short sides with a ½" (13mm) seam allowance. Fold the strip in half crosswise, lining up the seams, and notch at the top and bottom of the fold.

Attach the Fabric to the Frame

6. With the right side of the fabric facing you, line up the notches with the marks on the cornice, aligning the seams in the fabric with the corners of the cornice. Wrap the fabric around the cornice and temporarily "pin" it to the underside with upholstery tacks, smoothing the fabric with your hands as you work.

7. Staple the fabric to the underside and top of the cornice, stapling at the middle on each side along its width, followed by the edges on each side along its height. Continue stapling along one short side, followed by the other. Then move on to one long side followed by the other (A). When you approach a corner, turn the fabric under on the diagonal, as in the back of an envelope (B). Remove the upholstery tacks. Trim away excess fabric.

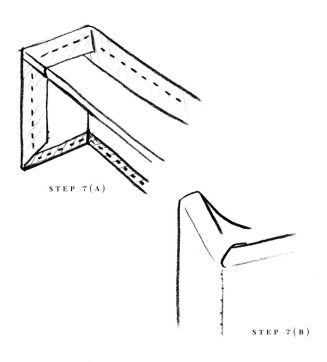

STEP 7(A)

STEP 7(B)

8. To line the inside of the cornice, drape the drapery lining over the top of the cornice and onto the underside. Fold the raw edges under on the top of the cornice and staple along the edge. Staple the fabric to the underside of the cornice wherever two pieces of wood meet (A), trim the fabric, and fold the raw edges under to create a finished look. Repeat for the inside edges (B).

Mount the Cornice

9. The cornice should be positioned so that it covers the top of the window casing but does not extend more than 5" (13cm) above it. With school chalk, mark the center of the cornice and the center of the window just above the window molding. Line up the marks, and attach the returns to the wall with the L brackets and the 2" (5cm) #6 wood screws.

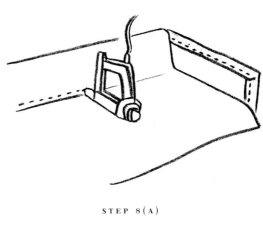

STEP 8(A)

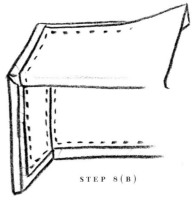

STEP 8(B)

TRICK OF THE TRADE >>>

The key to making a professional-looking cornice is in the tension. If you are working with patterned fabric or one that has a very obvious grain, keep the tension consistent and the grain straight. The best way to do this is to constantly smooth the fabric, allowing your hands to glide easily across it—not stick to it—to manage the tension.

RELAXED *roman* SHADE

IN UPHOLSTERER AND DECORATOR PARLANCE, relaxed shades are so named not for how simple they are to make, but rather for the relaxed way they hang in the window. This is achieved with a system of rings without rods, as opposed to the rings with rods used in the constructed Roman shade, which add weight and assist the folding. The relaxed, flat style is easier to make, and, like all Roman shades, works well with patterned fabrics.

Perhaps the most important step in making this shade is measuring the window on which it is to be hung. If your window is not the same width across the top and bottom (often the case in older houses), use the smaller measurement when calculating your shade size.

MATERIALS

- 3 yd (2.7m) upholstery fabric
- 5 yd (4.5m) lining fabric, including enough to cover the header
- 32" (81cm) long ⅜" (10mm) dowel
- 34" length of ⅜" (10mm) fabric tubing
- Fringe adhesive
- 33¾" (86cm) long 1 x 2 (2.5 x 5cm) board for the header
- Twelve brass-plated sew-on rings
- Four ¼" (6mm) screw (or microscrew) eyes
- 8 yd (288cm) ¹⁄₁₀" (1.4mm) lift cord
- 1 cord drop
- Four 2" (5cm) screws
- 4" (10cm) cleat with screws
- Basic upholstery tools (See page 15)

FINISHED MEASUREMENTS

- All materials are for a 33¾" (86cm) wide x 68" (173cm) long shade. Adjust according to the size of your window.

Measure and Cut the Fabric

1. Using a metal tape measure, take the dimensions of the window inside the casing. Measure across the top and the bottom and use the smaller measurement. For the length, measure from inside the top casing to the sill on the far right-hand and left-hand sides; again, use the shorter measurement. Our window measured 34" (86cm) from side to side and 68" (173cm) from top to bottom. To achieve the proper fit, subtract ⅛" (3mm) from each side of the width. This made our finished shade width 33¾" (86cm).

2. To determine the width of fabric to cut, add 5" (12.5cm) (two 2" [5cm] turnarounds and two ½" [13mm] seam allowances) to the finished shade width. For the length, add 9½–10½" (24–26.5cm) (a 2" [5cm] turnaround and a ½" [13mm] seam allowance on the bottom, plus 7–8" [18–23cm] for a wraparound header at the top) to the finished shade length.

The piece of fabric I cut for this shade was 38¾" (98.5cm) wide x 78" (198cm) long.

STEP 4

<<< TECHNIQUE TIP

If your window is wider than the one shown here, sew another brass ring between the two on the side seams at each level. This will prevent the shade from sagging when the shade is pulled up, or, as we say at The Furniture Joint, having too deep a smile. The ideal look for a relaxed shade is a shallow smile.

3. Using a metal yardstick and school chalk, mark the calculated dimensions on the right side of the fabric. Cut out. Repeat with the lining fabric.

4. With wrong sides together, place the lining on top of the fabric. Trim 2" (5cm) off each of the sides of the lining.

Sew the Shade

5. With right sides together, pin the sides of the lining and upholstery fabric together. Note that the lining is 2" (5cm) narrower on each side than the fabric. Machine-stitch both sides with a ½" (13mm) seam allowance. Turn the panel right side out. Fold in half lengthwise and notch the lining at the top and bottom of the fold.

6. Lay the panel, top side down, on a work surface. Smooth with your hands and measure the width at various intervals to make sure it is correct and uniform. Press along the side seams.

7. Slide the dowel into the fabric tubing. Glue the ends of the fabric tubing closed with the fabric glue. Slide the covered dowel between the two layers of fabric and pin the dowel in place 6" (15cm) from the bottom of the panel. The dowel will be sewn in place when the rings are attached in step 11.

8. Folding both the upholstery fabric and the lining, turn the bottom edge of the fabric under ½" (13mm) and then 2" (5cm) and pin to the lining. Topstitch the hem in place along the top edge of the fold.

Wrap the Header and Attach It to the Shade

9. Wrap the header with lining fabric, turning the raw edges under and stapling the folded edge over the raw edge on a wide side of the board. Fold the lining over the ends as if wrapping a gift and staple. Mark the center of the board with a pencil.

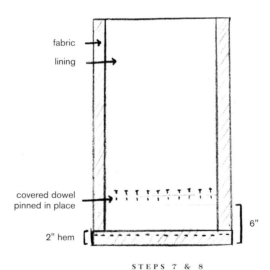

fabric

lining

covered dowel
pinned in place

6"

2" hem

STEPS 7 & 8

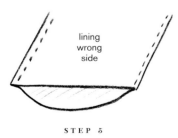

lining
wrong
side

STEP 5

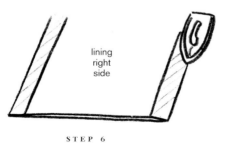

lining
right
side

STEP 6

STEP 9

10. Lay the shade lining side up on a work surface. Measure and mark 68" (173cm) from the bottom. Place the header staple side down on the panel, positioning it so that the top edge of the header is at the 68" (173cm) mark on the panel. Cut away all fabric above the top edge of the header in excess of 5" (12.5cm). Fold the fabric over the header, turning under the raw edge so that the finished edge aligns with the bottom edge of the header's back side. Staple along the edge.

Attach the Rings and Lift Cord

11. Measure and mark the fabric every 10" (25cm) along both side seams, beginning at the dowel. Hand-sew a brass-plated ring at each mark on the seam. Sew the rings on the seam at the top of the dowel so that you catch the tubing fabric that encases the dowel. Tie off the thread in a knot, and queeze a tiny dab of fringe adhesive on each knot to secure it.

12. Using a pencil, mark the horizontal and vertical center of the back of the header. Make 2 more marks along the middle of the header where it aligns with the side seams. Make a fourth mark in the middle of the header ½" (13mm) in from the right edge. Fasten the screw eyes on the header in the marked places.

13. Thread the lift cord through the rings according to the illustration. Starting on the bottom left of the shade, tie the end of a length of cord to the lowest ring. Thread the cord through the rings above it, across the top of the header through the center screw eye, followed by the 2 screw eyes on the right side of the header. Thread the loose end through the cord drop and knot. Repeat with rings on the right side of the shade, threading the cord only throughthe two screw eyes on the right side of the header. Thread the loose end through the cord drop and knot.

Mount the Shade

14. To mount the shade, position it in the window and screw through the underside of the header (the side containing the screw eyes) to the top of the window casing. Screw the cord cleat (see page 182) to the inside of the window casing, about one-third of the distance from the inside of the top casing.

FABRIC TIP >>>

> When pressing edges or seams with an iron, be aware that some fabrics will shrink if the iron is too hot. This is very common with silks, for instance.

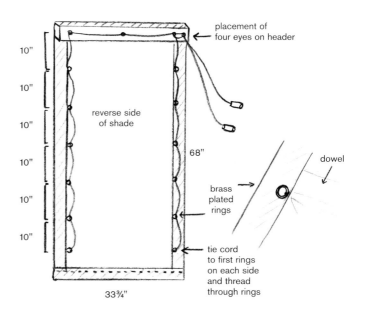

10"

10"

10"

10"

10"

10"

placement of four eyes on header

reverse side of shade

68"

33¾"

dowel

brass plated rings

tie cord to first rings on each side and thread through rings

STEP 13

STOOL WITH *drop-in* SEAT

SOMETIMES CALLED A SLIP SEAT, most upholstered pieces of this kind consist of a piece of plywood padded with foam and Dacron or some other kind of batting. Such is the case here, but you may discover on removing the upholstery and padding from your piece that the frame is actually open, with a webbed top covered by burlap. If the webbing is taut, leave it alone. If it is sagging or torn, remove it and replace the webbing and burlap (see page 190). Whatever style you're working with, the drop seat is generally screwed to the frame on the underside of the seat. Dining room and kitchen chairs are good examples of this.

{ before

Prepare the Seat

1. Strip the seat down to the frame (see Stripping Furniture, page 188).

2. Place the plywood form on the foam and, using a permanent marker and a metal yardstick, trace around the form, adding ½" (13mm) to all sides. Cut out foam piece (see Cutting Foam, page 192). The piece of plywood on our stool was 16" x 14" (40cm x35cm), so the cut foam was 17" x 15" (43cm x 38cm).

3. Spray 313 adhesive all over one side of the plywood form and on the top and sides of the foam. Wait about 2 minutes for the glue to become tacky, then set the plywood onto the foam, glued sides together. Make a rolled edge (see Making a Rolled Edge, page 193).

4. Drape the Dacron over the foam and staple to the bottom edge of the plywood using the Four-Point Tacking and Stapling Technique (page 189). Trim off excess, and mark the center front and center back of the seat with a permanent marker.

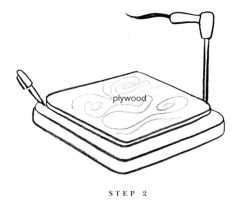

STEP 2

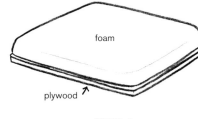

STEP 3

STEP 4

<<< PADDING TIP

Don't be tempted to use foam any thicker than 1½" (3.8cm) for a drop seat, or it will be impossible to smooth the puckers from the corners.

Keeping the tension of the fabric consistent is essential for a professional-looking job. If you pull the fabric too tight, you'll create unattractive indentations along the rolled edge. To achieve consistent tension in the fabric, draw your hand over it with minimal pressure as you staple, a bit like the way one pulls on a pair of panty hose. If you simply grab and staple, the tension will be uneven.

Measure and Cut the Fabric

5. To determine the dimensions of the fabric you need to cut, use a cloth tape measure to find the length and width of the padded seat from the bottom edge of the plywood to the opposite bottom edge. Add 2" (5cm) to each side for wrapping the fabric under.

    The fabric dimensions for our stool were 22" (56cm) wide x 20" (51cm) long.

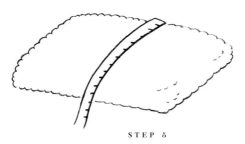

STEP 5

6. Using a metal yardstick and school chalk and with the fabric right side up, mark a rectangle on the fabric using your fabric dimensions, centering the design if desired. Fold the rectangle in half crosswise and notch at the top and bottom of the fold to mark the center. Then fold it in half lengthwise and repeat.

Cover the Seat

7. Stretch the fabric over the seat, right side up, lining up the center notches on the fabric with the center marks on the seat. Wrap the fabric to the underside of the plywood and, using the Four-Point Tacking and Stapling Technique (page 189, temporarily tack it to the underside of the plywood. You may need to hammer the upholstery tacks and remove them several times as you work around the seat to keep the fabric smooth and the tension consistent.

STEP 7

STEP 8

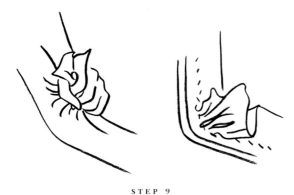

STEP 9

8. Staple the fabric to the underside of the plywood using the Four-Point Tacking and Stapling Technique (page 189), smoothing the fabric and keeping the tension consistent as you work. Remove the tacks as you go.

9. To make smooth corners from the flaps of fabric at the corners, pull each corner flap taut until there are no puckers in the corner, and staple or tack it to the underside of the plywood. Begin pulling and stapling or tacking on one side of the corner and work your way around to the other side.

Attach the Seat to the Stool

10. Drop the upholstered seat back into the stool or chair frame and fasten it using the existing hardware.

TECHNIQUE TIP >>>

If you are covering a set of chairs or stools with drop-in seats, number the chair and the seat to ensure that you reattach each seat to the correct stool or chair. While they may be part of a matching set, the way in which they were previously upholstered could be different from chair to chair.

KNIFE-EDGED *settee* PAD

THIS ALMOST FLAT CUSHION STYLE, in which a thin layer of foam is wrapped in Dacron, is designed to make wooden, rush, or caned chair seats more comfortable. It is so called because the edge of the cushion is crisp—sharp as a knife, so to speak—as opposed to rolled. The height of the pad can vary from 1" (2.5cm) to about 2" (5cm) high, depending on the style of the chair. To decide how high to make yours, consider the proportion of your piece—will the balance be thrown off with a too-thin or too-thick pad?—as well as a comfortable seat height.

{ before

MATERIALS

- 1 yd (91cm) cambric
- School chalk
- 1½–2 yd (1.4–1.8m) upholstery fabric, or more if patterned
- Dressmaker's pins
- Metal yardstick
- 22" x 45" (56cm x 114cm) piece 1" (2.5cm) LX45 blue foam
- Electric kitchen knife or hacksaw blade
- 74 adhesive
- 313 adhesive
- 1½ yd (1.4m) ½" (13mm) Dacron
- Machine-stitching thread in a complementary color
- 3½ yd (3.2m) complementary trim

FINISHED MEASUREMENTS

- All materials are for a 40" (102cm) wide x 20" (51cm) deep x 1½" (3.8cm) high seat cushion. Adjust according to the size of your settee or chair.

Make a Pattern

1. Drape a piece of cambric or muslin over the seat to be covered. Using school chalk, outline the seat along its front edge, sides, and the front of the back legs. Cut out the cambric or muslin pattern along the chalk line.

Cut Out the Fabric and Foam

2. Working with the fabric right side up, pin the pattern to it, centering the design motif if the fabric requires it. Using a metal yardstick and school chalk, trace the pattern onto the fabric, adding ¾" (2cm) all the way around (½" [13mm] for the seam allowance and ¼" [6mm] for the knife edge). Repeat to make a second panel, taking care to match the design of the first panel if it is patterned. The top and bottom panels of our seat pad measured 41½" x 21½" (105cm x 55cm).

3. Lay the cambric pattern on the foam and temporarily pin it down with a few pins. Outline the pattern onto the foam with a permanent marker. Cut the foam, adding ½" (13mm) on all edges (see Cutting Foam, page 192).

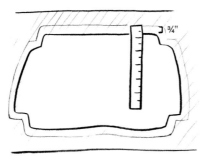

STEP 2

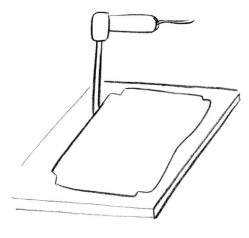

STEP 3

Create the Knife Edge

4. Spray the edges of the foam with 74 adhesive. When it is tacky (3–5 minutes), pinch together the edges all the way around the foam to create a knife edge.

5. Spray one side of the foam with 313 adhesive and wait 2 minutes for it to become tacky. Drape the Dacron over the foam, smoothing it with your hands to ensure it adheres, and trim to fit it exactly to the foam. Flip the foam over and repeat on the other side. Make sure to glue the edges of the Dacron together. Set aside.

Sew the Cover

6. With the right side of the top fabric panel facing up, pin the trim to the panel, with the raw edge of the trim ⅜" (10mm) from the raw edge of the panel. Machine-stitch the trim to the panel with a ½" (13mm) seam allowance (A). With right sides together, pin the top panel to the bottom panel. Machine-stitch the two pieces together with a ½" (13mm) seam allowance, beginning along the back edge, about one-third of the distance in from the side and ending on the back edge the same distance from the other side, leaving an opening to insert the pad. If you're using thicker foam, the opening will need to be slightly wider. Clip any corners (usually these are where the pad meets the seat's legs) on an angle (B).

7. Turn the cover right side out. Slide the foam pad in through the opening in the back, smoothing the fabric over the pad as you insert it. Hand-stitch (see page 194) the opening closed, turning the bottom panel (the panel to which the trim is not sewn) under ½" (13mm) for the seam allowance.

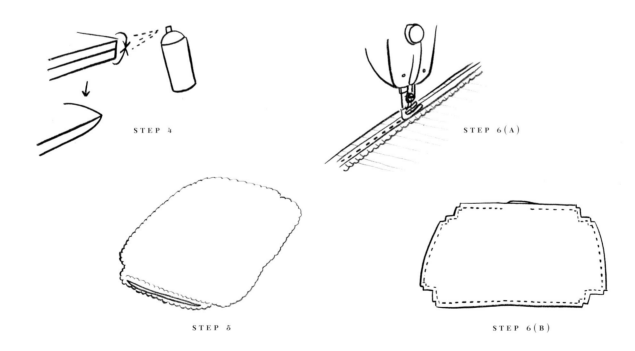

STEP 4

STEP 5

STEP 6 (A)

STEP 6 (B)

FLOOR *lounge* CUSHION

THIS STYLE OF CUSHION—a minimalist's version of the bean bag chair—
is among the most common. If you learn how to make this oversized one,
you will be able to make them for sofas, chairs, and ottomans. The basic
pieces of a box cushion include a top and bottom panel, a continuous
border that covers the front, sides, and a small portion of the back, and a
border that incorporates a zipper in the back. Because you will likely use
fabric that isn't wide enough to cut the continuous border in one piece,
you will need to stitch three lengths together (rather than two) so that the
seams fall on the sides of the cushion rather than in the front. The blue
foam required for this cushion is usually available in 24" (61cm) and
27" (68.5cm) widths, which necessitates gluing pieces together to make
a piece with larger dimensions. You can have the foam cut and glued to
your desired dimensions at a
specialty foam shop or by
a local upholsterer. I highly
recommend it, since patching
together your own can be
time-consuming and
painstaking.

MATERIALS

- 3 yd (2.75m) upholstery fabric
- Metal yardstick
- School chalk
- 42" (107cm) of continuous plastic zipper in a complementary color
- Dressmaker's pins
- Machine-stitching thread in a complementary color
- 36" (91cm) square 6" (15cm) thick LX35 blue foam; if having it cut professionally, dimensions are 35" x 35" x 6" (90cm x 90cm x 15cm) (1" [2.5cm] wider and deeper than the finished size)
- 74 adhesive
- Electric kitchen knife or hacksaw blade
- 313 adhesive
- 2½ yd (2.3m) ½" (13mm) Dacron
- Heavy-duty silicone lubricant

FINISHED MEASUREMENTS

- All materials are for a 34" (86cm) wide x 34" (86cm) deep x 6" (15cm) high floor cushion. Adjust according to the size you desire.

Measure and Cut the Seat Fabric

1. Using a metal yardstick and school chalk, measure and cut two 35" (90cm) square fabric pieces for the top and bottom pieces of the floor cushion; this includes ½" (13mm) on each side for seam allowances. Fold each panel in half and notch at the top and bottom of the folds to mark the center. Mark the back of each fabric piece with school chalk. Finish the edges of each piece with a zigzag stitch (see page 195). Set aside.

Make the Front Border

2. Measure three sides of the top panel to determine how long to make the continuous border. The border for our cushion measured 102" (259cm). Depending on the width of your fabric, cut one strip the entire width, then cut a second strip for the length that remains. This second strip will be cut in half and each half placed on one side of the long strip to avoid a seam in the front of the cushion. Then, once the border is sewn to the top and bottom panels, the excess material that remains in the back will be trimmed.

For this cushion, I cut two 7" (18cm) wide strips (for a 6" [15cm] thick cushion, plus ½" (13mm) on both sides for the seam allowance) across the full width of the 54" (137cm) fabric. Cut one strip in half crosswise. Fold the long strip in half crosswise and notch at the top and bottom of the fold to mark the center. Finish the edges with a zigzag stitch. With right sides together, pin one short piece to each end of the longer pieces and machine-stitch together with a ½" (13mm) seam allowance. Set aside.

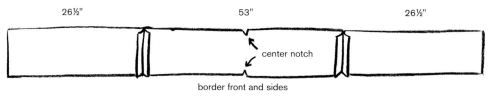

26½"   53"   26½"

center notch

border front and sides

STEP 2

NOTES ON PADDING

I've used foam to pad many of the projects in this book. There are three main types of foam. White foam, most commonly used by manufacturers who mass-produce furniture for retail, is the least expensive and has the shortest life span. LX blue foam, used in this book for all projects requiring foam, is more expensive but has a higher density and thus a longer life. Professional custom-upholstery studios use this for high-quality projects. The longest-lasting foam is made from natural latex. Most commonly found in such pieces as Eero Saarinen's womb chair, Arne Jacobsen's egg chair, and Hans Wegner's papa bear chair, as well as many Danish-style pieces, this type of foam has a rubbery feel to it. All of these foam types are available in soft, medium, and hard densities. Medium-density foam is generally used for seat cushions, whereas soft foam is used for back cushions. Hard foam is used more for commercial work, such as seating in restaurants. One final type of foam, called Ever Dry foam, allows water to pass through and hence is used exclusively for outdoor furniture.

For sofas, many of my decorators and customers choose to use foam-core, down-wrapped seat cushions. This consists of a soft-density foam wrapped in a casing of down and feathers. Down comes from the fluffy, bottom part of a goose; the more coarse and wiry feathers come from their wings. For back cushions, however, the favorite is all down and feathers. This is softer than a foam and down mix, but to prevent feathers poking through the cushions—a common problem—the mix of down and feathers needs to be correct. The correct mix for seat or back cushions is 60/40: 60 percent down, 40 percent feathers. The two parts work together to create the proper balance. If there are too many feathers and not enough down, nothing softens the feathers, and they will poke through the ticking of the cushion (the ticking is a covering made of strong fabric, usually cotton). If there is too much down, the cushion will pack together, reducing volume.

Because feathers are much cheaper than down, many companies mass-produce with a 25/75 blend or a 10/90 blend. Whenever you buy furniture containing down and feathers, unzip the cushion cover and check the blend on the label. Do not try to fix a cheap blend by inserting thicker ticking. The feathers and down need to be taken out, remixed with a proper balance, and blown in again. Just be warned: This procedure can be costly.

Make the Back Border

3. The back border will contain the zipper. Cut two strips of fabric at 7" (18cm) wide by 28" (71cm) long (the cushion will be 6" [15cm] high and 34" [86cm] long, and the front border wraps around 4" [10cm] on each side). Working with one strip at a time and with the wrong sides together, fold each strip in half lengthwise. Pin the zipper to the folded strip with the fold meeting the center of the zipper teeth and the cut ends aligned. Machine-stitch the closed zipper to the strip, stitching it as close to the fold as possible (A). With the wrong side of the zipper facing you, trim away the top layer of fabric, using the edge of the zipper as a guide (B). Finish the edges with a zigzag stitch. Repeat with the second strip on the other side of the zipper. This piece is now the back border of the cushion. Fold this back border in half crosswise and notch at the top and bottom of the fold to mark the center.

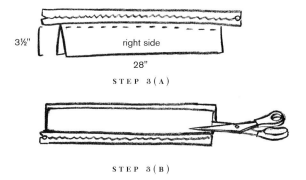

3½"   right side

28"

STEP 3(A)

STEP 3(B)

Assemble the Cushion

4. With right sides together, line up the notches on the continuous border and at the front of the seat and pin the border to the seat. Beginning at the front notches, machine-stitch the border to the top panel with a ½" (13mm) seam allowance. As you approach the corners, stitch to just beyond ½" (13mm) away from the edge, leaving the needle down. Clip the corner on an angle. Raise the presser foot and pivot the fabric 90 degrees, then continue stitching the next side of the border to the top panel. Make sure the seams joining the border pieces lie open as you stitch over them. Since the border joins the zipper on the back edge, continue stitching down that side to the next corner and stitch approximately 2" (5cm) on the back border . Flip the border and top of the cushion over and, again beginning at the center front notch, stitch the other side. Machine-stitch the bottom panel to the border in the same way.

5. To sew the zippered back border to the top and bottom panels, with right sides together, line up the notch on the back of the top panel with one of the notches on the back border. Beginning at the notches, machine-stitch the back border to the top panel with a ½" (13mm) seam allow-ance, ending 2" (5cm) short of where the back border meets the continuous border. Flip the whole thing over and repeat on the other side, again beginning at the notches. Repeat on the bottom panel.

<<< TRICK OF THE TRADE

A note on fabrics: Because this cushion is likely to be a favorite of kids and pets, use a hard-wearing fabric such as canvas or denim. Pre-wash it and press while damp before cutting it. Likewise, use synthetic rather than metal zippers for all cushions. Not only is metal weaker, but it is rough against the fabric and can cause "pulls" in some fabrics, especially those with an obvious weave.

6. Join the zipper piece to the continuous border by overlapping the ends and snipping into both layers of fabric where the fabrics meet (A). Line up the snips and machine-stitch the overlapping fabrics together with a ½" (13mm) seam allowance. Repeat on other side. Finish machine-stitching the border to the top and bottom panels (B).

7. Turn the cover right side out. Using the sharp end of a tufting needle, pull out the corners.

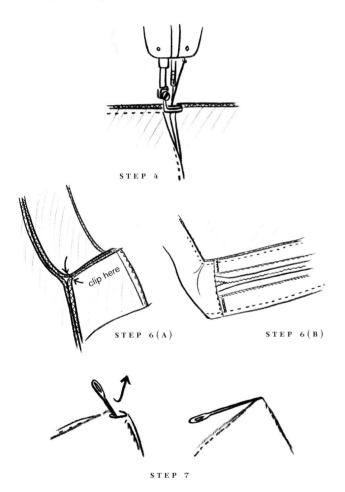

STEP 4

clip here

STEP 6(A)   STEP 6(B)

STEP 7

Prepare the Foam

8. To make the foam insert, cut a 35" x 35" x 6" (90cm x 90cm x 15cm) piece of foam (1" [2.5cm] wider and deeper than the finished size). If you are constructing your own insert, glue several pieces of foam together with 74 adhesive, marking the dimensions desired with a permanent marker. Cut the foam (see Cutting Foam, page 192).

9. Spray the top of the foam and the bottom of the Dacron with the 313 adhesive. Wait 2 minutes for it to become tacky, then drape the Dacron over the top of the foam (do not apply Dacron to the sides). Cut away the excess Dacron. Flip the foam over and repeat on the bottom. Then cut a 6" (15cm) strip of Dacron to cover the front edge (do not apply Dacron to the zipper or side edges) and glue it to the front of the foam and the front edges of the top and bottom pieces of Dacron.

Finish the Cushion

10. Pull the cover over the insert. Slide your hand around the inside of the cover and pull the seams so that they're flat against the border.

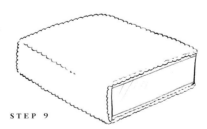

STEP 9

HALF-*skirt* SLIPCOVER

THINK OF THIS AS A SLIPCOVER for a dining room chair. It's not fixed or permanent, making it a good choice if you want your dinner table to serve as a place for both casual family meals and formal entertaining. What's more, it allows for a bit more leeway with fit than an upholstered chair does, though the cover won't look its best if it's too loose or too tight. Make the cover any length you like, from a mini skirt like the one pictured here to a maxi skirt that almost hits the floor. When determining the length of your skirt, measure from the point at which the seat panel ends and the vertical seat back begins.

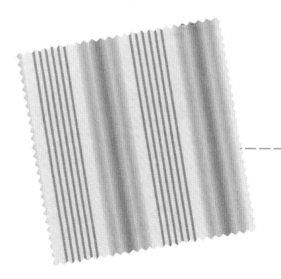

MATERIALS

- 3 yd (2.7m) lightweight fabric
- Upholstery pins
- School chalk
- 3 yd (2.7m) upholstery fabric
- Dressmaker's pins
- Machine-stitching thread in a complementary color

FINISHED MEASUREMENTS

- All materials are for a 20" wide x 18" deep (51cm x 46cm) seat pad with a 6" (15cm) long skirt. Adjust according to the size you desire.

Make a Pattern and Cut the Seat Fabric

1. Make a pattern for the seat by draping a piece of lightweight fabric across the seat and pinning it in the center. Using school chalk, outline the shape of the seat, using the outer edge of the chair frame as your guide. Trace around the inside of the back uprights of the chair and any other parts of the back that impact the shape of the seat (A). Add ½" (13mm) on each side of the pattern and cut out (B). Fold the seat pattern in half lengthwise and trim the pattern so that it is symmetrical. Lay the pattern on the right side of the upholstery fabric, mark with school chalk, and cut out. Fold the seat fabric in half lengthwise and notch at both ends of the fold to mark the center. Set aside.

2. Cut out four 2" x 10" (5cm x 25cm) strips of upholstery fabric for the back ties. Set aside.

Make the Skirt

3. Add twice the depth of the seat to the width to determine the dimensions of the front of the skirt (the front and side panels). For the 3 sides of our chair's border, the front and side panel of the skirt measured 56" (142cm) wide. Because it is likely that your upholstery fabric will be less than 56"

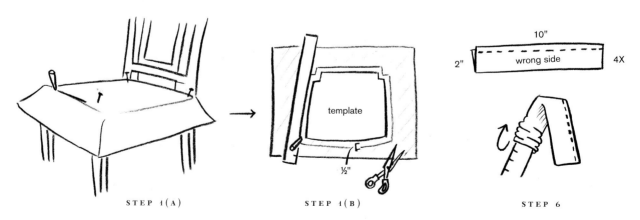

STEP 1(A)   STEP 1(B)   STEP 6

(142cm) across, you'll need to cut two lengths of fabric, each twice the depth of the skirt plus 1" (2.5cm) (two ½" [13mm] seam allowances). The strips for our skirt were 13" (33cm) long (twice the finished length, plus 1" [2.5cm] for seam allowances). Cut these 2 strips across the roll of the fabric from selvedge to selvedge. Fold one strip in half crosswise and notch at the top and bottom of the fold to mark the center. Fold the second strip in half crosswise and cut along the fold.

With right sides and short ends together, machine-stitch the three panels together with a ½" (13mm) seam allowance, matching the design motifs if working with a patterned fabric. Do not trim the excess fabric; it will be used to make the skirt's corner pleats (each is 2½" [6.5cm] deep, using 5" [12.5cm] of fabric).

4. Mark and cut the back strip of the skirt the width of the chair back, measuring from the outer edge of each back leg, plus 1" (2.5cm) for the seam allowances (use the same length measurement as for the front and side skirt piece). Our chair back was 18" (46cm) across, so our back strip was 13" (33cm) long x 19" (48cm) wide.

5. With wrong sides together, fold the skirt panel—the front and side panels—in half lengthwise and pin together along its length. Machine-stitch the raw edge (along the long side only) with a ½" (13mm) seam. With wrong sides together, fold the back strip in half lengthwise and pin together along its length. Machine-stitch the raw edge along the long side only with a ½" (13mm) seam allowance. Press along the folds.

6. Fold one of the strips cut in step 2 in half lengthwise with right sides together. Machine-stitch together the raw edges of one short side and the long side with a ½" (13mm) seam allowance. Using a pencil, turn the strip right side out. Pull out the corners with a sewing needle. Fold the remaining raw edge under ½" (13mm) and topstitch closed. Repeat with the remaining 3 strips.

FABRIC TIP >>>

Pleats can be tricky, so for your first attempt, it may be a good idea to avoid pattern matching by choosing a solid fabric.

Attach the Skirt to the Seat

7. To prevent fraying, zigzag-stitch around the perimeter of the seat border. Cut into the inner corner of each upright ½" (13mm) and sew the edges around the uprights under ½" (13mm) (A). With right sides together and the raw edges aligned, pin the skirt to the front and sides of the seat panel, lining up the front notch of the seat panel with the notch on the skirt. Make inverted pleats at the front corners of the seat by folding the fabric onto itself to make two pleats, each 2½" (6cm) deep, facing each other (B). A patterned fabric may need more or less than 2½" (6cm) of fabric folded back to match the pattern. Pin the pleats and try the skirt on over the chair before stitching it to be sure the pleats are aligned with the corners. Adjust as necessary. Beginning at the center front notch, machine-stitch one side of the skirt to the seat with a ½" (13mm) seam allowance. Flip over and repeat on the other side, again beginning at the center front notch.

8. With right sides together and the raw edges aligned, pin the back strip of the skirt to the back of the seat panel, lining up the notches. Machine-stitch together with a ½" (13mm) seam allowance.

9. To attach the ties to the cover, insert one into the top of the opening on one side of the skirt and sew the entire opening closed, turning ½" (13mm) of the raw edges inside. Sew another tie into the back skirt in the same way, then repeat for the other back corner. Topstitch the ties in place and the openings closed.

Finish the Seat Cover

10. Zigzag-stitch all of the raw edges on the underside of the seat cover machine to prevent fraying.

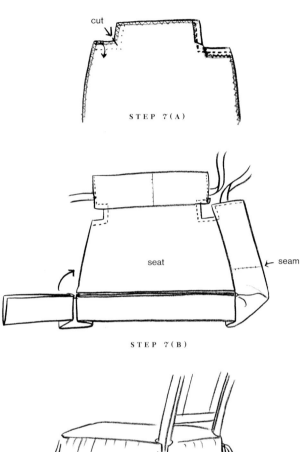

cut

STEP 7(A)

seat

seam

STEP 7(B)

STEP 9

BUCKRAM-TOPPED *curtains*

FULL-LENGTH CURTAINS are a decorator favorite because their look complements the clean, modern yet casual interiors so popular right now. Buckram, a stiff cotton fabric, is used here to reinforce the top of the curtains, where the hooks are inserted. Buckram is sold by the yard on a roll, so you'll need to buy 3 yards of 4"- (10cm-) wide buckram if you'll be making the curtains pictured. Be sure to mount the decorative rod before you take any measurements, as its placement determines the finished length of the drapes.

Determine Dimensions

1. Mount the rod above the window molding before determining the finished dimensions of your drapes. Use a level to make sure the rod is straight. The rod should be wider than the casing (the decorative wood that surrounds a window and gives it a finished look). Place the rings on the rod. Using a tape measure, measure the distance between the bottom of the rings and the floor. Our window measured 108" (274cm) from ring to floor. Next, measure the width of the window from one outer edge of the casing to the other outer edge. Our window was 42" (107cm) wide. Depending on how full you want the drapes to be, the width of the curtains should be double or triple the width of the window. I like drapes to form a gentle S-curve (as seen from above), generally achieved by doubling the width of the window— that is, by making each drapery panel (since you'll be making

HOW TO MEASURE A WINDOW

When a customer calls to ask if I can give them an estimate for curtains, I ask them to provide me with the window measurements first. Nine times out of ten, the other end of the line goes silent. Indeed, figuring out where to place the tape measure (inside the casing? at the top of the casing?) is not obvious to the novice sewer. So, if you're making sill-, apron-, or floor-length curtains for a sash window, follow these simple guidelines and use a steel tape measure:

To measure the finished *length*, measure from the bottom of the rod to the sill for an apron-length curtain, to the bottom of the apron or lower sash for a sill-length curtain, and to the floor for floor-length curtains.

To measure the finished *width*, measure from outside edge to outside edge of the window frame, then add 6" (15cm) to each side for a rod with no return; if the rod has a return, add the depth of the return to each side.

two) the full width of the window. Each of our finished panels were 108" (274cm) long x 42" (107cm) wide.

Measure and Cut the Fabric

2. Determine the length of the upholstery fabric to cut first: Add 3" (7.5cm) (two ½" [13mm] seam allowances and a 2" [5cm] hem) to the finished length of the curtain (see step 1). To determine the width, add 5" (12.5cm) (two 2" [5cm] turnarounds and two ½" [13mm] seam allowances) to the finished width of the curtain.

I like to give myself a little extra room on the length, since stitching the fabric to the lining tends to pull it up. This is especially true of linens, silks, and sheers. I usually add about 10" (13cm) or so. Each of our panels was 125" x 47" (317.5cm x 119cm).

3. Using a metal yardstick, a square, and school chalk, mark two panels using your determined dimensions on the right side of the upholstery fabric and cut them out. If you need to join two lengths of fabric, cut them so that the design motifs match and the top seam will be in the same place across the two panels.

4. From the lining fabric, cut two linings the same length of the panels but 4" (10cm) less than the width of the panels.

TECHNIQUE TIP >>>

The looseness of the gather in your curtains depends on how far apart you space the pinch pleat hooks. The farther apart they are, the looser the gather.

Sew the Curtains

5. With right sides together, pin the sides of the fabric and lining together (the lining will be narrower than the fabric). Machine-stitch them together along each side with a ½" (13mm) seam allowance to within 4" (10cm) of the bottom. With the curtains wrong side out and the lining side facing you, press along the sides. Since the upholstery fabric is wider than the lining, 2" (5cm) of the fabric will wrap around to the back on both sides.

6. Machine-sew along the top of the curtains with a ½" (13mm) seam allowance. Place the bottom edge of the buckram along that stitch and align the ends with the sides of the curtains. Pin in place. Machine-sew the buckram to the curtain as close to the bottom edge of the buckram as possible (A). Turn the curtain right side out and smooth the top of the curtain with your hands. Topstitch through the lining and fabric, just below the bottom edge of the buckram, across the entire width of the curtain (B).

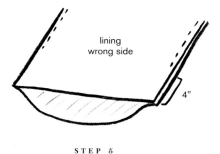

lining
wrong side

4"

STEP 5

7. Measure and mark the drape at the desired finished length. Add 2" (5cm) to this measure and trim away the excess. Zigzag-stitch (see page 195) the raw edge of the upholstery fabric to prevent it from fraying when you turn it under; repeat for the lining edges. Turn 3" (7.5cm) of the lining under, pin, and machine-sew as close to the raw edge as possible. Turn the curtain fabric under 2" (5cm), pin, and machine-sew as close to the raw edge as possible.

Attach the Hooks and Hang the Curtains

8. Lay the curtains on a work surface with the lining facing you. Using a metal yardstick and pins, mark the panel along the top every 5–6" (12.5–15cm) across and 1¾" (4.5cm) below the top edge of the curtain. Attach the pinch pleat hooks to the curtains at each mark, inserting them through the lining and the buckram but not through the fabric (despite the name, unless your drapes are pinch pleats, the hooks are not inserted into pleats). Hook the curtains to the rings on the rod.

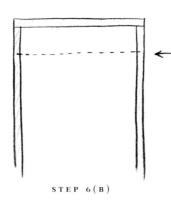

STEP 6(A)   STEP 6(B)

TECHNIQUE TIP >>>

All pinch pleat hooks should be inserted into the top of the curtains so that, when hung, the uppermost part of the hook falls ¼" (6 mm) below the top edge of the curtain.

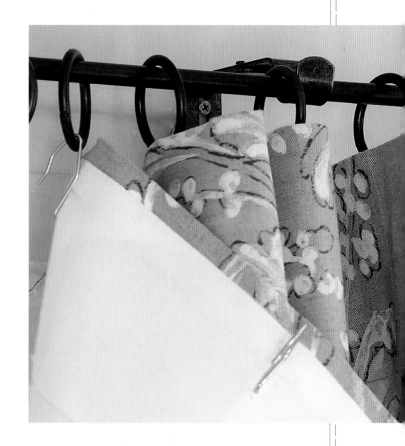

FRINGED *cube-shaped* POUF

MY NOW TWO-YEAR-OLD SON, Jaden, learned to walk by pulling himself up using this short ottoman and then pushing it around the living room! Consider this project a preliminary course in fully upholstered sofas and chairs. The upholstered pouf is essentially a small-scale version of those larger projects, since the fabric is stapled to the frame and the pieces are attached using tacking strip—both marks of an upholstered piece.

{ before

MATERIALS

- ½ yd (46cm) 1½" LX45 blue foam, if necessary
- 74 adhesive
- 2½ yd (2.3m) ½" (13mm) Dacron
- 2½ yd (2.3m) upholstery fabric
- 4 yd (3.7m) ¼" (6mm) cardboard tacking strip
- ½ yd (46cm) cambric
- 2½ yd (2.3m) decorative trim in a complementary color
- Basic upholstery tools (See page 15)

FINISHED MEASUREMENTS

All materials are for an 18" (46cm) cube-shaped pouf. Adjust according to the size of your stool.

Prepare the Frame

1. Strip the stool to the frame (see Stripping Furniture, page 188).

2. If replacing the foam, cut an 18" (46cm) square piece of foam (see Cutting Foam, page 192). Spray one side of the foam and the top of the stool with the 74 adhesive and wait 3–5 minutes for it to become tacky. With the glue sides together, place the foam on the top of the stool. Roll the edges (see Making a Rolled Edge, page 193).

3. Drape the Dacron over the foam and staple just above the marks where the fabric was previously attached, using the Four-Point Tacking and Stapling Technique (page 189) and shooting the staples in on an angle. Trim away the excess.

Measure and Cut the Fabric

4. To determine how much fabric you need for the top of the stool, measure the distance across the top of the stool, from the bottom edge of the Dacron on one side to the other. Add 2" (5cm) to each side. For our stool, the distance between one edge of the Dacron to the other was 18" (46cm). The

STEP 4

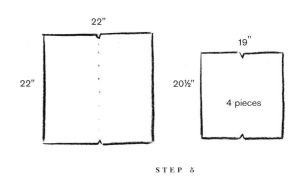

STEP 5

dimensions of the fabric for our top, then, were 22" (56cm) square. To calculate how much fabric to cut for the sides, measure from the top edge of the stool to the bottom edge and from side to side. Add ½" (13mm) for the seam allowances on the top and the two sides and 2" (5cm) on the bottom for wrapping underneath the stool. The sides of our stool measured 18" (46cm) square, so I cut 4 pieces of fabric each 19" (48.5cm) wide x 20½" (52cm) high.

5. Lay the fabric out on a work surface right side up. Using a metal yardstick and school chalk, mark and measure the fabric in the calculated dimensions, centering the design motif if using a patterned fabric. Cut out all 5 pieces. Mark the right side of each piece of fabric with school chalk. Fold each piece in half lengthwise and notch at the top and bottom at the fold to mark the center.

Attach the Top Panel to the Frame

6. Using a permanent marker, mark the center of each side of the stool at the top and bottom. With the right side facing you, drape the top piece of fabric over the Dacron, lining up the notches in the fabric with the marks on the sides

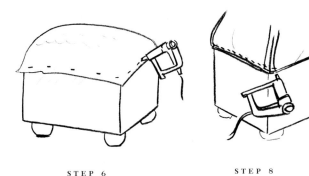

STEP 6   STEP 8

TRICK OF THE TRADE >>>

Use the tacking hammer to gently tap the top corners where you have stapled the tacking strip so that they don't stick out—they should be flush with the sides of the stool.

of the stool. Temporarily "pin" the fabric around the sides of the stool about 1" (2.5cm) below the top edge with upholstery tacks and the magnetic hammer, using the Four-Point Tacking and Stapling Technique (page 189). Smooth the fabric with your hand constantly as you "pin" the fabric down. Staple the fabric to the sides of the stool about 1" (2.5cm) below the top edge, using the four-point tacking and stapling technique and continuously smoothing the fabric with your hand.

Attach the Border to the Frame

7. With right sides together, pin the four pieces of the border together along their sides. Machine-stitch them together with a ½" (13mm) seam allowance, creating a 4-sided tube.

8. With the border inside out, slide it onto the stool so that the notches on the border line up with the notches on the top panel. Staple the border in three places on each square of fabric: in one top corner, in the center, and in the other top corner. Make sure the seams lie open on the corners before stapling. Make sure the design motifs on the top and sides line up, if applicable, by pulling the fabric down with the right side out. Repeat this stapling method on all sides.

9. With the border still inside out, staple the tacking strip along the stool's top edge, just below the top edges of the sides, keeping the staples straight and close together.

10. Wrap the sides of the stool with Dacron, positioning it just above the tacking strip and stapling it into the tacking strip using the Four-Point Tacking and Stapling Technique (page 189). Wrap the Dacron onto the bottom side edge of the stool and staple using the same technique. Trim away excess.

11. Pull the border onto the sides of the stool by pulling it down a few inches (4–8cm) in one corner and working your way around to the other corners, making sure the seams line up in the corners (A). Using upholstery tacks, temporarily "pin" the fabric to the underside of the stool in the corners, then in the center on the bottom of each side. Continue pinning every 2" (5cm) around the underside of the stool. Using the Four-Point Tacking and Stapling

Technique (page 189), staple the fabric in place and remove the upholstery tacks. Trim excess fabric. Staple tacking strip over the raw edge of the fabric (B).

Finishing

12. With the stool underside up, drape a piece of cambric over the bottom and trim to within an inch of the frame. To trim around feet, cut into the cambric from the corner on an angle. Turn 1" (2.5cm) of the cambric under and staple to the frame, using the Four-Point Tacking and Stapling Technique (page 189).

13. Hand-stitch the trim (see page 194) around the bottom edge of the stool, working your way around the perimeter. Cut the trim in the back so that it is flush with the other end, and hand-stitch the ends together. Depending on the type of trim, you may choose to hot-glue or staple it instead.

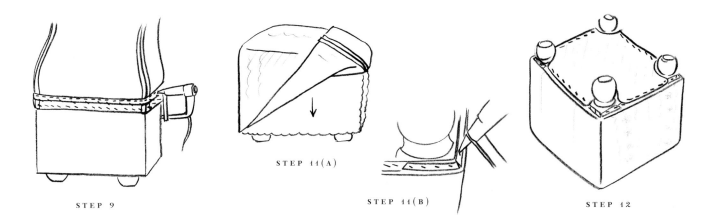

STEP 9   STEP 11(A)   STEP 11(B)   STEP 12

WHAT TO LOOK FOR IN A FLEA MARKET FIND

When I first opened The Furniture Joint, I spent a lot of time looking for forlorn sofas and chairs that could benefit from an expert upholstery job. I never paid more than $50 for any piece, no matter the provenance, and I always did a thorough investigation of the furniture before handing over my money.

What should you look for? The first step should always be a visual sizing-up, checking for extraordinary form, good bones, and maybe even a sought-after name in furniture design, though a pedigree is not always necessary. Next you need to get closer to the chair—practically intimate, in fact! Poke your fingers into the padded crevices between backs and seats, politely shake the piece to determine if the arms or legs wobble, then put your hand up through the underside, if possible. Finally, take a seat. If the spring action is less than comfortable, the problem could be worn webbing on the underside, which allows the springs to push out through the bottom. A piece with this problem will need to be stripped to the frame, repadded, and recovered. If the springs are uneven up through the top of the seat, it is a sign that the binding twine tying each spring has broken. This also means a full stripping of the frame will be required. And that squeaking sound? It is common in pieces made with zigzag springs (often found in inexpensive furnishings) that have ripped out of the frame. The noise is the result of worn rubber coating on the EK clips that hold the springs in place. Again, this piece would need complete stripping. If that nice plump cushion on a piece you're eyeballing sinks deep into the sofa or chair when you sit in it, it could mean that the seat is supported by elastic webbing that's lost its elasticity. Strip this piece to the frame, too. If there are no problems with the springs, check the padding. When you give the cushioning a squeeze, does it feel like you're crushing crackers? This is a sign that the padding has dried out and the piece should be stripped to the frame. If the padding is intact, you've likely landed a piece that simply needs new fabric.

BOUDOIR *stool*

THIS IS A GOOD PROJECT for learning how to expertly upholster curved pieces of furniture. Rounded edges let you practice maintaining consistent tension in the fabric—the key lies in pulling the fabric just right to avoid pleats and puckers. Round pieces, with very few exceptions, have low seats and are never heavily padded for this very reason. As with any upholstery, the more you work on curved pieces, the more natural the feeling becomes.

{ before

MATERIALS

- ½ yd (46cm) cambric
- 21" (53.5cm) square 2" (5cm) LX45 blue foam
- Electric kitchen knife or hacksaw blade
- 74 adhesive
- 313 adhesive
- ½ yd (46cm) ½" (13mm) Dacron
- ½ yd (46cm) upholstery fabric
- ½ yd (46cm) trim
- Basic upholstery tools (See page 15)

FINISHED MEASUREMENTS

All materials are for a round stool with a 20" (51cm) diameter. Adjust according to the size of your piece.

Prepare the Frame

1. Strip the stool down to the frame (see Stripping Furniture, page 188).

2. If replacing the foam, make a pattern for it by draping a piece of cambric over the frame and outlining it around the edge of the frame using school chalk. Add ½" (13mm) all the way around for the rolled edge and cut out. Place the cambric on the piece of foam and trace around it with a permanent marker. Cut the foam (see Cutting Foam, page 192).

3. This particular stool had a removable wood form. Spray the top and sides of the foam as well as the top of the form with 74 adhesive. Wait 3 to 5 minutes for the glue to become tacky, then, with the glue sides together, place the foam on the top of the form. Roll the edges to create a crown seat (see Making A Rolled Edge, page 193).

4. Spray the foam all over with 313 adhesive. Wait 2 minutes until tacky, then drape a piece of Dacron over the foam and staple it to the bottom side edge of the form using the Four-Point Tacking and Stapling Technique (page 189).

STEP 4

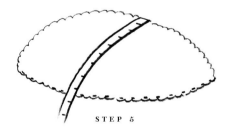

STEP 5

<<< TECHNIQUE TIP

The maximum height of a round form on a stool like this should be 2½" (6.5cm) (2" [5cm] foam plus ½" [13mm] thick plywood). If the combination of plywood and foam is any thicker, it will be difficult to smoothly wrap the fabric to the underside of the form, and you will end up with puckers.

Measure and Cut the Fabric

5. Using a cloth tape measure, measure the diameter of the padded form from the bottom edge of the form to the opposite bottom edge. Our stool measured 20" (51cm). To determine how much fabric to cut, add 4" (10cm) to the diameter (for wrapping the fabric under) and cut a square with sides that length. For our stool, I cut a 24" (61cm) square piece of fabric.

Attach the Fabric to the Frame

6. Drape the fabric over the Dacron and pin on the edges of the foam in 4 places equidistant from each other, smoothing with your hand to make sure the tension of fabric is consistent. Using upholstery tacks, temporarily "pin" the fabric around the circumference of the form, smoothing with your hand as you work.

7. Leaving the tacks in place, stretch the fabric to the underside of the form and "pin" with upholstery tacks in 4 places equidistant from each other and then tack the fabric all the way around. Staple the fabric to the underside about 1" (2.5cm) in from the edge, shooting the staples on an angle and about ½" (13mm) apart. Remove the tacks as you staple around the form. Trim the excess fabric.

Finishing

8. With the form top side down, staple the trim to the underside, positioning it with the decorative edge just beyond the bottom edge of the form. Shoot the staples on an angle about ⅛" (3mm) apart. To join the ends of the trim, cut them so that they meet without overlapping, then hot glue the ends and staple them to the underside of the form. Set the seat into the frame and fasten.

TRICK OF THE TRADE >>>

When an instruction calls for temporary tacking or stapling, avoid driving tacks or staples into the frame by tilting the stapler so that the staples go in on an angle. If using tacks, drive them in on an angle.

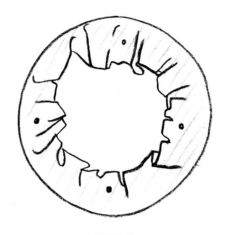

STEP 7

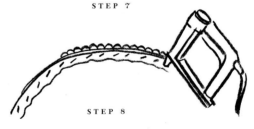

STEP 8

FABRIC TIP >>>

Don't use striped fabric for this project. Because the frame is circular, the lines will become distorted as the fabric is stretched into place.

advanced

Step into my studio on any given day and you will find me working on a project similar to those in this chapter. The mix of pieces here is designed to stretch your skills— you'll learn how to attach webbing to a rounded edge and how to transform plain fabric into something a bit more special using biscuit tufting and French-stitching. Though very different in approach—tufting requires pulling twine through the fabric and all of the padded layers to the support below, whereas French-stitching involves hand-stitching through the fabric only—they both create a decorative pattern on the fabric, a hallmark of upholstered furniture. You'll also learn how to handle that ever-popular yet not-so-simple-to-work-with fabric, leather. One of the overarching lessons comes from projects with more challenging tension than in the two previous chapters:

In such projects as the Upholstered Headboard (page 150) and Cushioned Library Chair (page 144), you will not be wrapping the fabric underneath the frame, so the technique for smoothing the fabric correctly is a subtle yet essential one.

Perhaps the most intriguing—and difficult—project here is the one that my students are both enamored and mystified by. How *do* you attach that last piece of fabric on the outside back of a fully upholstered chair? When I reach this step in the instruction, there always seems to be a collective *aha!* I trust that you will respond exactly the same way. And the gratification that comes with achieving what I like to call the PhD in this course will only inspire you to continue learning about the art of upholstery. That certainly has been the case for me.

THREE-PANEL *folding* SCREEN

THIS SCREEN CONSISTS OF three fully covered panels, each with two faces and a border. I used the same patterned fabric for the front and back here, but I have made many for clients using different fabrics for the front and back so that it can be used as a room divider rather than simply for decoration or to hide things behind. If you choose patterned fabric, pay extra close attention when cutting it (see Measure Twice, Cut Once, page 186) if you'd like the panels to match up when hinged together.

<<< FABRIC TIP

Measure and Cut the Fabric

1. To determine the length of the pieces of fabric you need, add a ½" (13mm) seam allowance and 2" (5cm) for stapling on the bottom to the finished height of the panel. For the width, add two ½" (13mm) seam allowances to the finished width of the panel. For our screen, I cut 6 panels of fabric, each 74½" (189cm) long x 19" (48.5cm) wide.

To determine the length of the borders, double the height and add the width of the top. Then divide by 2 and add ½" (13mm) on each side for seam allowances and 2" (5cm) for wrapping under. Add two ½" (13mm) seam allowances to the finished width to determine the width of the borders. For our borders, I cut 6 strips, each 2" (5cm) wide x 84" (213cm) long.

2. To match the pattern of the fabric as we did, cut 2 front panels first. Using a metal yardstick and school chalk, measure and mark the first panel along one selvedge edge. Cut this panel out and use it as a guide to matching up the pattern on the opposite side of the fabric, folding the edge under ½" (13mm) before lining up the pattern, then measure and mark the fabric ½" (13mm)—to allow for the seam—beyond where the pattern lines up. Cut out the second panel. Use this panel as a guide to cutting out the third panel, matching up the patterns as described above.

STEP 2

Cut the 3 back panels using the same pattern matching method. Number all panels on the wrong side with school chalk. Fold each panel in half lengthwise and notch at the top of the fold to mark the center.

Repeat this process to cut out 6 border strips, matching the pattern at the short ends.

Sew the Fabric Covers

3. With right sides facing, machine-stitch 2 border strips together along the short sides with a ½" (13mm) seam allowance. Repeat with the remaining pairs of border strips.

4. Working on one set of panels at a time, with right sides together, pin the border to the front panel, lining up the seam on the border with the notch at the top of the panel. Note: The border covers only the top and sides of the panel. Machine-stitch the front panel to the border with a ½" (13mm) seam allowance. Pin the back panel to the border, right sides together, in the same fashion as above and machine-stitch. Turn right side out. Repeat with the remaining panels and borders.

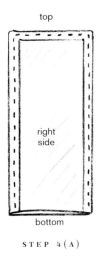

top

right
side

bottom

STEP 4(A)

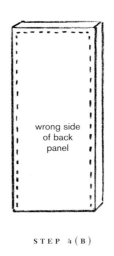

wrong side
of back
panel

STEP 4(B)

Prepare the Frame

5. If the frame is solid wood or solid but hollow, like a door, you will only need to wrap it in Dacron. If it is a frame only, attach plastic webbing to both sides of each panel to fill in the center of the frames (see Attaching Webbing to a Frame, page 190) (A). Drape a length of muslin over the webbing and trim to within 1" (2.5cm) of the frame. Fold the muslin under and staple it to the frame, using the Four-Point Tacking and Stapling Technique (page 189) and spacing the staples on an angle 1" (2.5cm) apart. Repeat for both sides of each panel (B).

6. Working with one panel at a time, spray one side with 313 adhesive. Wait 2 minutes until tacky, then drape the Dacron over the panel, staple it to the panel around the perimeter, and trim the excess Dacron. Do not cover the sides in Dacron. Repeat on the back side of the panel, then cover the remaining panels in the same fashion. Spray each panel all over with silicone lubricant.

Attach the Fabric to the Frame

7. Slide the fabric covers onto the panels, pulling them taut. Wrap the fabric at the bottom under, smoothing the panel as you pull it taut. Staple the fabric to the bottom edge of the frame, beginning in the middle, working to the left and then to the right. Trim excess fabric. Hammer a glide at each end of the bottom of each screen.

8. Attach the hinges 12" (30.5cm) from the top and bottom of the frames, flanking the middle frame.

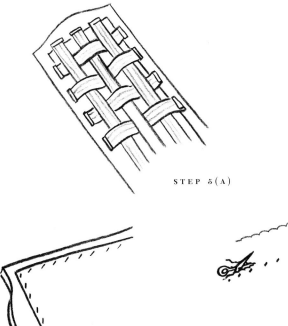

STEP 5(A)

STEP 5(B)

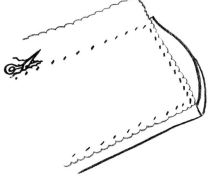

STEP 6

STEP 7

BISCUIT-*tufted* BENCH

A GREAT WAY TO ADD INTEREST to plain fabric, tufting creates an attractive grid of dimples that gives any furniture a bit of panache. Once strictly associated with nineteenth-century furniture, tufting was revived by twentieth-century modernists such as Mies van der Rohe, who began using biscuit tufting without buttons attached on his Barcelona chairs. Achieved by pulling strong twine through the seams of the fabric and padding beneath it, then stapling the twine to the plywood frame, tufting is well worth learning once you've mastered measuring, cutting, and machine-stitching. I strongly suggest you purchase a start-up tufting kit from Rochford Supply, Inc., an invaluable online resource (see Resources, page 200).

{ before

- 15½" x 20½" (39.5cm x 52cm) piece 2" (5cm) LX45 blue foam

- Electric kitchen knife or hacksaw blade

- 1½ yd (1.4m) upholstery fabric

- Hand drill with ½" (13mm) bit

- Steel-backed razor blades

- 313 adhesive

- ½ yd (46cm) ½" (13mm) Dacron

- Silicone spray lubricant

- 2½ yd (2.3m) tufting twine, cut into 6 equal lengths

- Basic upholstery tools (See page 15)

FINISHED MEASUREMENTS

- All materials are for a 20" (51cm) wide x 15" (38cm) deep x 2½" (6.5cm) high cushion. Adjust according to the size of your bench or sofa.

<<< TECHNIQUE TIP

Because the tufting twine is the last thing to be secured, make sure it does not make its way back through the holes in the plywood and get caught between the fabric and the foam as you are upholstering the cover to the plywood. You can drive an upholstery tack near the hole and wrap the twine around it to secure it temporarily.

Prepare the Frame

1. Strip the piece down to the frame (see Stripping Furniture, page 188).

2. Cut the LX45 foam ½" (13mm) longer and wider than the finished measurement (see Cutting Foam, page 192). It should be ¼" longer and wider than the plywood seat base.

3. Using a metal yardstick and a pencil, measure and mark a grid of squares on the plywood seat base. For our bench, I marked the plywood off in twelve 5" (12.5cm) squares.

Measure and Cut the Fabric

4. Use your marked square dimension plus 1" (2.5cm) (½" [13mm] on each side for seam allowances) for the fabric squares that will make up the top panel of the bench. For our bench, I cut twelve 6" (15cm) fabric squares.

5. Measure, mark, and cut out two 5" (12.5cm) wide strips of upholstery fabric (2" [5cm] for the height of the foam, ½" [13mm] for the plywood height, one ½" [13mm] seam allowance, plus 2" [5cm] to wrap underneath the plywood) across the roll of fabric for the border. The width of the fabric doesn't matter, since you will be cutting off any excess. With wrong sides together, stitch the border strips together along one short side with a ½" (13mm) seam allowance.

Sew the Cushion

6. Pin the squares right sides together in strips of 4 pieces, making sure the pile goes in the same direction. Machine-stitch together with ½" (13mm) seam allowances. With right sides together, pin the 3 strips together along the long sides, lining up the seams. Machine-stitch together with ½" (13mm) seam allowances. Press all seams open. Fold the sewn top in half lengthwise and notch at the top and bottom of the fold to mark the center.

7. With the right sides of the top panel and border together, line up the seam on the border with one of the notches on the side of the top panel, aligning the raw edges and making sure that the pile on the border brushes down (when it's right side out). Pin the border to the panel. Beginning at the notch, machine-stitch together with a ½" (13mm) seam allowance, making sure the seam of the border lies open as you sew. As you approach a corner, stitch to within ½" (13mm) of it, leaving the needle down. Clip the corner on an angle. Raise the presser foot, pivot the fabric 90 degrees around the needle, then sew along the next side. Sew to within 2" (5cm) of the notch on the other side. Repeat on the other side, beginning at the notch and ending within 2" (5cm) of the notch on the other side.

8. To join the ends of the border, trim away excess fabric to within a few inches (4–8cm). Overlap the ends of the border and notch through both layers where the pieces overlap. With right sides together, line up the notches and machine-stitch the ends together with a ½" (13mm) seam allowance. Machine-stitch the opening between the border and the top panel closed.

Attach the Cushion to the Frame

9. Place the plywood on a work surface, grid side up. Drill holes at each intersection of the grid using a ½" (13mm) drill bit.

10. Using a permanent marker, measure and mark a grid on the foam (cut in step 2) that replicates the one on the plywood. Using a razor blade, score an X into the foam, about ½" (13mm) deep, at each grid intersection.

11. Spray one side of the plywood and one side of the foam all over with 313 adhesive. Wait 2 minutes until tacky, then place the foam glue side up on a work surface. Place the plywood glue side down on top of the foam. The foam should extend ¼" (6mm) beyond than the plywood all the way around.

12. Wrap the foam and plywood with the Dacron, stopping at the side of the bottom edge of the plywood. Staple the Dacron to the plywood, beginning in the middle of one side and working to the left and then to the right. Repeat on the remaining 3 sides. Using a razor blade, cut X-shaped slits through the Dacron where the holes in the foam are. Spray the Dacron all over with silicone lubricant.

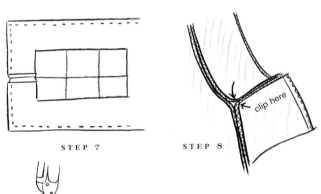

STEP 7

STEP 8

clip here

STEP 9

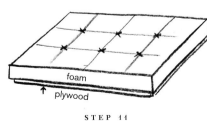

foam

plywood

STEP 11

STEP 12

Tuft the Cushion

13. Thread one 38" (96.5cm) piece of twine through the tufting needle, doubling up the thread. Beginning on the underside of the cover at the intersection of four of the squares, stitch through both thicknesses of the seam, stitching on the diagonal (A). Bring the needle down through the padding—through the Dacron, foam and plywood, leaving about 6" (15cm) free (B). Repeat with the remaining holes.

14. Fit the border over the edges of the padded plywood. Stuff quarter-sized pieces of Dacron in the corners to make them crisp and square. Staple the raw edges of the border to the underside of the plywood, using the Four-Point Tacking and Stapling Technique (page 189). Measure as you go to maintain 2½" (6.5cm) height. Trim away the excess fabric.

Finishing

15. With the underside of the cushion facing you and beginning in the center holes, pull both ends of one piece of twine at a time to achieve the desired depth of tufting on top, making sure each tuft's tension is consistent. Staple the twine to the plywood adjacent to the hole. Reinforce the staples by stapling again, doubling the twine back on itself, and stapling another time.

16. Screw the cushion into the frame on the underside, or fasten it in the fashion it had previously been attached.

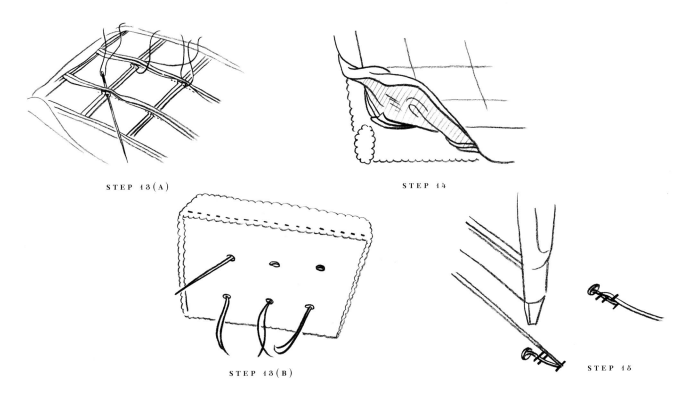

STEP 13(A)

STEP 14

STEP 13(B)

STEP 15

FRENCH-STITCHED *window* SEAT

MAKING THIS HANDSOME CUSHION is much like making the
Floor Lounge Cushion on page 94. It differs in a few ways, however:
There is no zipper, lengths of rolled Dacron are tucked along the
seams to create an edge, and French-stitching is employed to give
those edges a decorative structure. The resulting cushion looks far
more decorative than, say, a pillow or a plain box cushion, and is
particularly well-suited to a window seat.

French-stitching is both functional and decorative, however,
since it gives structure to the edge of cushions and mattresses and,
unlike a normal hand-stitched seam, is
meant to be seen. I generally like to
use a ⅛" (3mm) stitch and a narrow
angle, which results in stitches that
are closer together.

MATERIALS

- 2 yd (1.8m) upholstery fabric
- 30" x 20" (76cm x 51cm) piece 5" (12.5cm) LX35 blue foam
- 313 adhesive
- 2 yd (1.8m) ½" (13mm) Dacron
- Silicone spray lubricant
- 5" (13cm) curved hand-stitching needle
- Bonded 69 nylon machine thread (hand-stitching twine) in complementary color
- Basic upholstery tools (See page 15)

FINISHED MEASUREMENTS

All materials are for a 40" (101.5cm) wide x 11" (28cm) deep x 4" (10cm) high cushion. Adjust according to the size of your window seat or bench.

Measure and Cut the Fabric

1. To determine the length and width of the top and bottom panels, add two ½" (13mm) seam allowances and one ½" (13mm) allowance for the French-stitch to the corresponding finished dimension of the panel. For the border height, add two ½" (13mm) seam allowances and one ½" (13mm) allowance for the French-stitch to the finished border height. For the border length, add 1" (2.5cm) for the two ½" (13mm) seam allowances to the perimeter of the top panel. The top and bottom panels for our cushion were 41½" x 12½" (105.5cm x 32cm) and the border was 5½" (14cm) high and 103" (61.5cm) long.

2. Place the fabric right side up on a work table. Using a metal yard stick and school chalk, measure and mark the dimensions of your top and bottom panels on the fabric. Cut out. Fold each panel in half crosswise and notch at the top and bottom of the fold to mark the center. Mark the back of each panel with school chalk.

3. Since the border is longer than the width of the fabric, cut two 6" (15cm) wide strips across the roll. Fold one in half crosswise and cut in half along the fold. Fold the other strip in half crosswise and notch at the top and bottom of the fold to mark the center. With right sides together, pin one end of each short piece to the ends of the long piece and machine-stitch with a ½" (13mm) seam allowance.

<<< **TECHNIQUE TIP**

The wider apart the French stitches, the deeper the angle at which you bring the thread up through the fabric and the fewer stitches you need to make. This is the most expedient way to French-stitch, but personally, I prefer closer stitches for a more professional look.

Sew the Fabric

4. With right sides together, line up the notch on the border with the notch at the front of the top panel and pin the two together (A). Beginning at the front notch, machine-stitch the border to the top panel with a ½" (13mm) seam allowance. As you approach a corner, stitch to within ½" (13mm) of it, leaving the needle down. Clip the corner on an angle. Raise the presser foot, pivot the fabric 90 degrees around the needle, and sew along the next side. Stitch to within 4" (10cm) of the back notch. Repeat on the other side: Beginning at the center front notch, stitch the other side to within 4" (10cm) of the back notch. Join the border by overlapping the ends, clipping into both layers of the fabric where they line up with the notch on the panel (B). Line up the notches and machine-stitch the border together with a ½" (13mm) seam allowance. Trim off the excess fabric and machine-stitch the opening between the border and the top panel closed with a ½" (13mm) seam allowance.

5. Machine-stitch the bottom panel to the border using the same method as for the top panel, leaving a centered 20" (51cm) opening in the back.

6. Turn the cover right side out. Using the sharp end of a tufting needle, pull out the corners.

7. Topstitch along the seams on the top and bottom panels, staying as close to the seam as possible. On the bottom panel, do not topstitch over the 20" (51cm) opening.

8. Using school chalk and a metal yardstick, mark the top and bottom panels 1" (2.5cm) in from the edge.

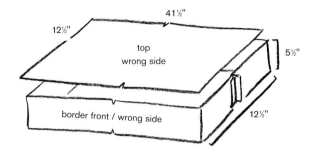

41½"

12½"

top
wrong side

5½"

border front / wrong side

12½"

STEP 4(A)

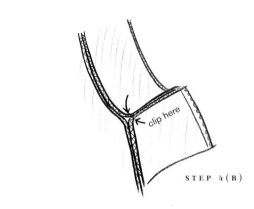

12½"

clip here

STEP 4(B)

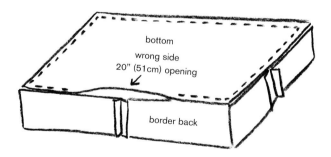

bottom
wrong side
20" (51cm) opening

border back

STEP 5

E FOOD • MICHEL GUÉRARD • DANISH FAMILY PIG FARM • ISAN THAI COOKING • SANCERRE • CALIFORNIA ROLL

Preserves, I often say, endear absents.—Charles Lamb

halves of the same apple. — Dorothy Draper

S SHOW YOU HOW

APRIL/MAY

Prepare and Insert the Padding

9. Spray the top and sides of the piece of foam with 313 adhesive. When it is tacky (2 minutes), drape the Dacron over the top and sides and smooth to adhere. Trim the excess. Flip the foam over and spray the bottom with 313 adhesive and adhere more Dacron to it. Spray the cushion all over with silicone lubricant.

10. Slide the padded foam into the cover. Roll Dacron into four 40" (101.5cm) long x 1" (2.5 cm) thick tubes, four 11" (28cm) long x 1" (2.5cm) thick tubes, and four 4" (10cm) long x 1" (2.5cm) thick tubes. Slide the tubes into the corresponding seams, rolling them as tightly to the seams as possible. Pin in place.

11. Hand-stitch the back opening closed. Finish the topstitching by hand.

French-Stitch the Cushion

12. To French-stitch, thread the curved needle with hand-stitching twine, tying a slipknot on the long end. Working on one edge of the cushion at a time and beginning on the inside top edge of the roll, bring the needle up through to the top of the cushion along the inside edge of the roll on an angle. Make a ⅛" (3mm) stitch and bring the needle straight down, back through to the inside edge. Bring the needle back up through to the top of the cushion on the same angle and again, and make a ⅛" (3mm) stitch on the top. Continue stitching around the cushion in this manner on both the top and bottom edges.

13. When the seam is entirely stitched closed, wrap the thread around the needle once or twice and make a tiny stitch into the fabric, holding the thread firmly near the point at which you inserted the stitch. Pull the needle back toward you to produce a knot that will secure your stitches.

14. Repeat the French stitches along the bottom panel and then along each edge of all four sides of the border.

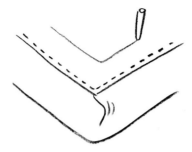

STEP 8

STEP 10

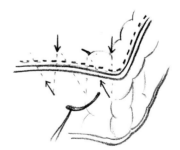

STEP 12

CUSHIONED *library* CHAIR

IT'S A GOOD IDEA to have upholstered another curved piece before embarking on this project, since it involves not only working with the fabric to avoid puckers but also attaching it to the frame while making sure the seat height is consistent all the way around.

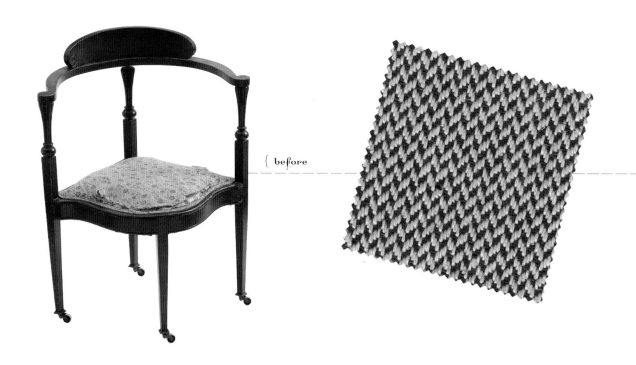

{ before

MATERIALS

- 4 yd (3.7m) jute webbing
- 2 yd (1.8m) tacking strip
- ½ yd (46cm) burlap
- ½ yd (46cm) cambric
- 20" (51cm) square 1½" (3.8cm) LX45 blue foam
- Electric kitchen knife or hacksaw blade
- 74 adhesive
- ½ yd (46cm) ½" (13mm) Dacron
- 1 yd (91cm) upholstery fabric
- 250 Z nails (decorative nails)
- Basic upholstery tools (See page 15)

FINISHED MEASUREMENTS

- All materials are for a 16" x 16" (40.5cm) corner chair. Adjust according to the size of your piece.

Prepare the Frame

1. Strip the chair down to the frame (see Stripping Furniture, page 188).

2. Place the chair on its back on a work surface. Attach webbing to the inside edge of the seat frame (see Attaching Webbing to a Frame, page 190) so that the webbing is flush with the top edge of the frame. Work the jute along the curve so that it sits smoothly on top of it (A). Before you staple the jute back onto itself, staple a length of tacking strip along the inside edge of the chair on top of the stapled jute using ¾" (2cm) staples. Now fold the jute back and staple (B).

3. Turn the chair right side up and drape a length of burlap over the webbing. Staple it to the inside edge of the frame using the Four-Point Tacking and Stapling Technique (page 189). Fold the excess onto itself and staple to the inside edge of the frame. Trim the excess.

Make a Pattern for the Foam

4. To make a pattern for the foam cushion, lay a piece of cambric over the burlap and, using school chalk, trace around the edges of the burlap. Cut out. Lay the cambric pattern on the foam and trace with a permanent marker. Cut the foam (see Cutting Foam, page 192).

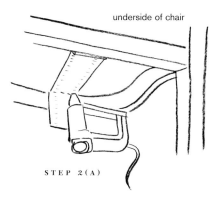

underside of chair

STEP 2(A)

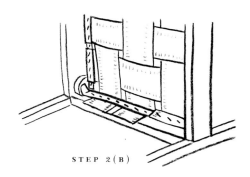

STEP 2(B)

Attach the Foam

5. Spray the burlap and bottom of the foam all over with 74 adhesive. Wait about 5 minutes until tacky, then place the foam on the burlap, glue side down.

6. Drape a length of Dacron over the foam and staple it to the inside edge of the frame using the Four-Point Stapling Technique (page 189). Trim away the excess.

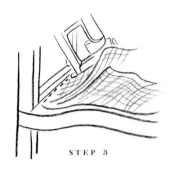

STEP 3

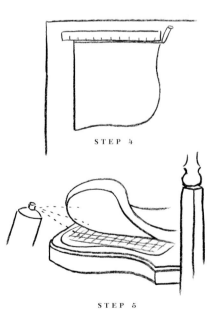

STEP 4

STEP 5

Cut Out the Top Panel

7. Use the same pattern you used to cut out the foam to make the top panel of the seat. Pin the pattern to the right side of the upholstery fabric and cut out, adding ½" (13mm) all the way around for the seam allowance. Fold the panel in half lengthwise and notch at the top and bottom of the fold to mark the center.

Measure and Cut the Border

8. To determine the width of the border fabric, add together the 1½" (3.8cm) thickness of the foam, one ½" (5cm) seam allowance and 2" (5cm) for stapling under. To determine the length, add two ½" (13mm) seam allowances to the perimeter of the foam cushion.

Because the fabric I used is railroaded (see page 186), I cut the border in one 58" (147cm) long x 4" (10cm) wide piece, so I needed to accommodate only one seam. If your fabric doesn't allow you to cut a single strip, cut two and add ½" (13mm) for the second seam.

Fold the border in half crosswise and notch at the top and bottom of the fold to mark the center.

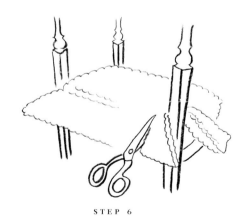

STEP 6

Sew the Fabric

9. With wrong sides together, line up the front notch on the top panel with the notch on the border and pin the border to the panel. Beginning at the notch and stopping 2" (5cm) from the end of the strip, machine-stitch the border to the top panel with a ½" (13mm) seam allowance, cutting notches into the fabric at the curves to prevent puckering. Repeat on the other side. Join the ends by overlapping them and notching where they overlap. Line up the notches and machine-stitch the border together with a ½" (13mm) seam allowance. Finish stitching the border to the top panel.

Attach the Fabric to the Frame

10. Fit the cover over the padded frame and pin it in place. Pull the seams so that they lie against the sides. Do

<<< **FABRIC TRICK**

When tacking the fabric down, be sure to leave enough space for the decorative nails—if there's not enough room for them, the nails will push up against the border and you'll lose its vertical lines.

not allow them to lie open. To fit the cover in the corners around the uprights, cut into the border on an angle to accommodate them. Trim away excess fabric, using the edge of the frame as your guide.

11. Using upholstery tacks and a tacking hammer, temporarily "pin" the cover to the frame, turning the fabric under as you go and spacing the tacks 2" (5cm) apart. Using a ruler, measure the height of the border as you work, making sure that it is 1½" (3.8cm) all the way around.

12. Pull the fabric gently along the border so that the seam rolls to the front. You don't want it to sit up on the edge of the padded cushion.

Finishing

13. Using a nylon-tipped tacking hammer, hammer in the Z nails, placing them so that they're touching. Remove the tacks as you work around the chair.

14. Turn the chair upside down. Drape a length of cambric on the underside. Trim to the edge of the frame. Tuck the edges of the cambric under and staple them to the frame, cutting the cambric on an angle at the legs to fit around them.

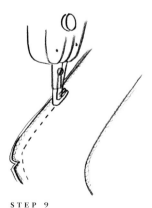

STEP 9

STEP 10

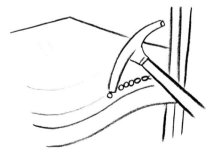

STEP 13

TRICK OF THE TRADE >>>

The trick to hammering decorative nails is to use a punching motion—strike them and bring the hammer back quickly. If you drive them in with a prolonged strike, you'll bruise the nail.

UPHOLSTERED *headboard*

I ADDED THE UPHOLSTERED INSET to this headboard—originally it was all wood. At first glance, this project may look like it belongs in the "Easy" category. What could be so challenging about stapling a piece of fabric to a headboard? Well, since the padding is very shallow and the fabric is not wrapped around anything, it is especially tricky to smooth the fabric and keep it taut. As you work, smooth the fabric constantly with your hands to achieve a professional look.

{ before

<<< PADDING TIP

Stick with foam that is no more than 1½" (3.8cm) thick for a headboard such as the one pictured. With thicker foam, the corners will not be smooth—they'll pucker when you try to tack the fabric to the headboard.

Determine the Foam Dimensions

1. To determine the dimensions of the piece of foam you need, subtract ⅛" (3mm) from the width and height of the headboard (or, as in our case, the inset). Fit the foam onto the headboard to be sure that once you roll the edges in step 2, there will be ¼" (6mm) of space between it and the headboard edge to tack the fabric and trim to the headboard. The foam for our headboard was 35⅞" (91cm) wide x 15⅜" (39cm) high and 1" (2.5cm) thick.

Attach the Foam to the Headboard

2. Spray the top and all of the side edges of the foam with 74 adhesive, as well as the area of the headboard you are covering. Wait 3 to 5 minutes for the glue to become tacky, then place the foam glue side down on the headboard. Roll the edges (see Making a Rolled Edge, page 193).

3. Drape the Dacron over the foam and staple it to the frame around the rim of the foam using the Four-Point Tacking and Stapling Technique (page 189), smoothing the Dacron as you staple around the frame.

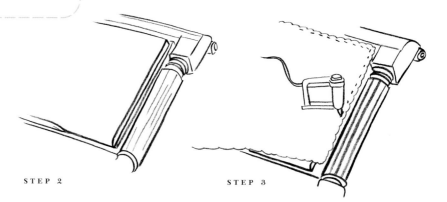

STEP 2   STEP 3

Measure and Cut the Fabric

4. To determine the dimensions of the piece of fabric you need to cut, add 2" (5cm) to each of the finished measurements. Our dimensions were 38" x 17½" (96.5cm x 44.5cm).

5. Using a metal yardstick and school chalk, measure and mark the fabric dimensions on the right side of the fabric. Cut out.

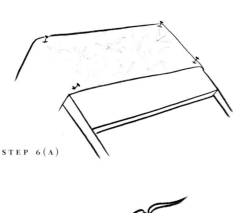

STEP 6(A)

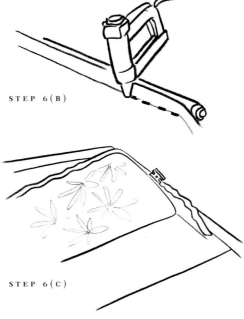

STEP 6(B)

STEP 6(C)

Attach the Fabric to the Foam

6. Lay the fabric over the Dacron and temporarily "pin" it to the headboard ⅛" (3mm) in from the edge with upholstery tacks, spacing them ½" (13mm) apart and using the Four-Point Tacking and Stapling Technique (page 189) (A). Smooth the fabric with your hands as you tack it down. It will be difficult to get the fabric to lay perfectly flat unless you vigilantly smooth the fabric. You may also need to remove and retack in places as you work around the headboard to achieve consistent tension. Staple the fabric in place, following the marks from the previous fabric, if any (B). Remove the tacks and trim away the excess fabric.

Finishing

7. Beginning in the middle at the bottom of the headboard, hot glue the trim to the headboard, covering the staples. Cut the end so that it is flush with the opposite end. Hot glue one end over the other so that the join is undetectable.

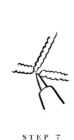

STEP 7

FULL *slipcover*

ONCE YOU'VE GRASPED THE INTRICACIES of measuring, marking, and cutting, you're ready to make a full slipcover such as this one. There is very little in the way of tools and materials involved—no webbing, no foam, no tacking or stapling—but plenty in the way of taking exact measurements and cutting patterns. The key is to fit the slipcover over the chair each time you stitch pieces of it together to make sure it is fitting properly.

{ before

MATERIALS

- 3 yd (2.75m) cambric
- School chalk
- 3½ yd (3.2m) upholstery fabric
- Dressmaker's tape measure
- Dressmaker's pins
- Machine-stitching thread in a complementary color

FINISHED MEASUREMENTS

- All materials are for a 17" (43cm) wide x 17" (43cm) deep x 42" (106.5cm) high dining chair. Adjust according to the size you desire.

—————————— <<< **FITTING TIP**

A full slipcover like this one works best for chairs that have little to no rise in the seat; if there is a rise, the slipcover can appear ill-fitting.

Make a Pattern for the Chair Seat and Back

1. For the front panel of the chair back: Set the chair on its back and drape a piece of cambric over the front of the chair back (A). Mark the outline of the back on the cambric with school chalk. Cut out, adding ½" (13mm) for the seam allowance on each side.

For the seat: Set the chair on its feet and make a pattern for the seat using the same method, pinning the cambric to the seat. At the front corners, make an inverted pleat and mark with the chalk so that when you open up the pleat, the outline accommodates the corners (B). Mark the cambric along the back edge where the uprights meet the seat. Cut out, adding ¼" (13mm) for the seam allowance on each side and an additional ¼" (6mm) along the back edge to provide flexibility so that when a person sits down on the seat, there's a little give.

For the back panel of the chair back (not including the skirt): Turn the chair onto its front legs. Use the pattern for the front panel of the chair back as a guide to making a pattern for the back panel of the chair back. Place the pattern on the back and add ½" (13mm) for the seam allowance plus the appropriate amount of length so that the back and skirt will meet. For our chair, I added ½" (13mm) to reach the skirt.

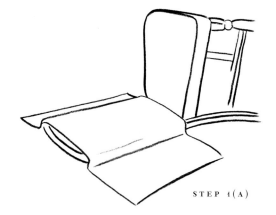

STEP 1(A)

STEP 1(B)

Determine Side Dimensions

2. To determine the width of the border for the side and top of chair back, add 2" (5cm) to the width of the side of the chair back at its widest point. Our borders were 4" (10cm) wide. To determine the length of the side borders, add 3" (7.5cm) to the distance from the top of the chair back to the top of the seat. The added length gives you a little flexibility. Our side borders were each 24" (61cm) long. To determine the length of the top border, add two ½" (13mm) seam allowances to the length of the top of the chair back. The length of our top border was 17" (43cm).

Cut the Fabric for the Seat and Back Panels

3. Lay the upholstery fabric right side up on a work surface. Arrange the patterns for the seat, the front panel of the chair back, and the back panel of the chair back, lining up the design motifs as desired. Pin and cut out. Fold the front and back fabric of the chair back in half lengthwise and notch at the top and bottom of the fold to mark the center. Fold the seat in half crosswise and notch at the top and bottom of the fold to mark the centers. Measure, mark, and cut 3 strips of fabric in the dimensions of the 2 sides and the top border. For our chair, there were two 24" (61cm) long x 4" (10cm) wide strips and one 17" (43cm) long x 4" (10cm) wide strip. Fold the top strip in half crosswise and notch at the top of the fold to mark the center.

Sew the Seat and Back

4. With right sides together, stitch the front corners of the seat together with a ½" (13mm) seam allowance, making inverted pleats. Place the cover on the seat to make sure the corners line up. With right sides together, line up the notch on the back of the seat with the notch on the bottom of the front of the chair back and pin, lining up the design motifs. Machine-stitch with a ½" (13mm) seam allowance. Drape the piece over the chair to check the fit.

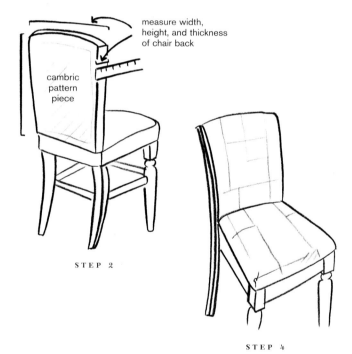

measure width, height, and thickness of chair back

cambric pattern piece

STEP 2

STEP 4

A FEW WORDS ABOUT FABRIC

All too often, I have to break the news to a customer that the fabric he or she spent months choosing is inappropriate for the piece of furniture to be upholstered. It is the least fun part of my work, because I have to start a relationship with a customer by saying no. But in the more than two decades that I've been practicing my craft, I have seen a sofa or two come into the shop with the absolutely wrong fabric covering it. So, before you spend anything on fabric, it's wise to talk to a professional to determine if you're headed for triumph—or disappointment. There is an exponential number of pairings of fabrics and furniture, but a few general rules may lead you in a safe and happy direction.

1. If the fabric has a brush or direction, such as velvet and corduroy, assess the style of furniture you want to put it on. Say, for example, that you want to cover an 84" (213cm) long sofa with three cushions and an upholstered back in a silk velvet that comes on a 54" (137cm) wide bolt. Because the velvet must all brush in the same direction, the back of the sofa has to consist of three pieces of the velvet seamed together. Do you want two seams running vertically on the back of your sofa?

2. Is your piece of furniture shapely? Avoid choosing stripes and bold patterns on curvaceous pieces (including the ever popular mid-century Danish modern egg and tulip chairs) since the lines of the furniture will warp the fabric. Stick to solids for these pieces to play up their extraordinary shapes.

3. Silks and linens are very popular, but on their own they won't stand up to the demands of upholstery. They must be backed with fusing or weft. Do not ignore this step, which can generally be requested when you order the material from the manufacturer.

5. With right sides together, pin a short end of each side border strip to the ends of the top border strip and stitch with a ½" (13mm) seam allowance. With right sides together, lining up the notches on the top border strip and the front panel of the chair back, pin the border to the panel. Beginning at the notch, machine-stitch with a ½" (13mm) seam allowance. As you approach the corner seam, stitch to within ½" (13mm) of it, leaving the needle down. Clip the corner on an angle. Raise the presser foot, pivot the fabric 90 degrees around the needle, then sew the next side. Make sure the seam on the border lies open as you stitch over it, and continue stitching along the side border. Repeat on the other side, beginning at the notch.

6. With right sides together, pin the back panel of the chair back to the border, lining up the notches on the top border and the back panel. Machine-stitch with a ½" (13mm) seam allowance, beginning at the notch. As you approach the corner seam, stitch to within ½" (13mm) of it, leaving the needle down. Clip the corner on an angle. Raise the presser foot, pivot the fabric 90 degrees around the needle, then sew the next side. Make sure the seam on the border lies open as

you stitch over it, and continue stitching along the side border. Repeat on the other side. Slide the cover over the chair to check the fit.

Determine the Skirt Dimensions

7. To determine the dimensions of the skirt, measure the perimeter of the seat and the height from the floor to the top edge of the seat. For the perimeter, use a cloth tape measure to measure from the center front of the seat to the center back of the seat. Double this measure. Our chair measured 34" (86cm) from center front to center back, so the total perimeter was 68" (172.5cm). For the floor height, drape the

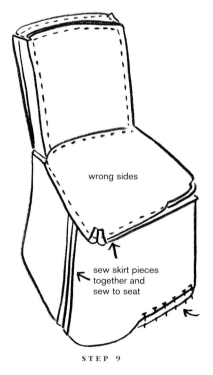

wrong sides

sew skirt pieces
together and
sew to seat

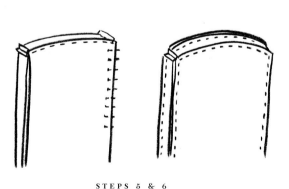

STEPS 5 & 6

STEP 9

seat fabric over the seat. Make a chalk line on the fabric where it hits the top edge of the seat frame. Using a metal yardstick, measure from the floor to the chalk line at the highest point of the seat. Our chair measured 18¼" (46cm) from the floor to its highest point.

Measure and Cut the Skirt Fabric

8. Cut your fabric at the height you just determined plus 3½" (9cm) (one ½" [13mm] seam allowance, a 1" [2.5cm] finished hem, and 2" [5cm] extra). The height of our skirt panel was 21¾" (55cm). To determine the width to cut, add 2" (5cm) (four ½" [13mm] seam allowances) to the seat perimeter. Split this number in half and cut two panels, since the skirt width will be wider than upholstery fabric. I cut two 36" (91cm) wide panels, including seam allowances. Measure, mark, and cut out the skirt panels, lining up the design motifs if desired.

Sew the Skirt

9. With right sides together, pin the short sides of the skirt pieces together. Machine-stitch with a ½" (13mm) seam allowance. With right sides together, line up the seams on the skirt with the notches on the sides of the seat and pin. Machine-stitch the skirt to the seat and back with a ½" (13mm) seam allowance.

Finishing

10. Place the cover on the chair to determine the length of the skirt, measuring from the floor up—not the seat down—and add 1" (2.5cm), marking all the way around the skirt with school chalk. Remove the cover from the chair. Cut along the chalk line. Turn ½" (13mm) of the bottom raw edge under, press, and turn under ½" (13mm) again. Pin. Topstitch the hem just under ½" (13mm) from the edge.

LEATHER *bureau* CHAIR

LEATHER UPHOLSTERY is among the most popular with my clients, probably because it ages so beautifully and gives instant cachet to anything it covers. It's durable, too, making it a good choice for oft-used furnishings like dining room chairs.

This project is geared toward chairs that have a box seat screwed onto a chair frame. Unlike a fixed chair seat, in which the pad and frame are one piece that you can't remove, the box seat can be detached from its frame with a screwdriver.

{ before

- 24 sq ft (7.3m) skin of leather or 1½ yd (1.4m) of fabric (see Measuring Hides, right)
- 4 yd (3.7m) of 4" (10cm) wide jute webbing for seating
- 1 yd (91cm) of 42" (106.5cm) wide burlap
- 2½ yd (2.3m) of 2" (5cm) thick fox edge
- Steel-backed, single-edge razor blade
- 74 adhesive
- One piece of 2" (5cm) LX35 blue foam, a little larger than the dimensions of the seat
- Electric kitchen knife or hacksaw blade
- 1 yd (91cm) of 24" (61cm) wide ½" (13mm) Dacron
- 4 yd (3.7m) of ready-made welting (optional)
- #3 and #7 tacks, if using magnetic tacking hammer
- 1 yd (91cm) 42" (106.5cm) wide cambric
- Basic upholstery tools (See page 15)

FINISHED MEASUREMENTS

- All materials are for an 18" x 20" (45.5cm x 51cm) box seat. Adjust according to the size of your seat.

Strip the Chair

1. Measure the height of the seat pad so that you can return it to that height when you reupholster it. Unscrew the seat pad from the chair.

2. With the underside of the seat facing you, strip the frame (see Stripping Furniture, page 188). The frame should be completely clean before you proceed.

Prepare the Frame

3. Place the frame top side up on a work surface. Attach the jute webbing (see Attaching Webbing to a Frame, page 190).

4. Lay a piece of burlap several inches (4–8cm) larger than the frame over the webbing. With the front of the frame facing you, staple the burlap to it using the Four-Point Stapling Technique (page 189), spacing the staples about ⅛" (3mm) apart. Finish the edge of the burlap by turning it onto itself and stapling it to the frame. Trim the excess.

5. Place the frame right side up with the front facing you. Working with the full length of fox edge and starting from the right corner, position it along the rim of the front of the frame with the flange facing in (see page 50 for more on a flange). Let the fox edge extend beyond the frame by ⅛" (3mm) and staple through the flange to the frame, working

<<< **FABRIC TIP**

The seat shown here is trimmed with ready-made welting (available at specialty trimming stores; see Resources, page 200). You don't have to use welting at all, but not only does it lend a crisp, finished look to the chair, it also strengthens the seat's seams. I used an upholstery-grade canvas welting rather than leather to avoid a thick, bulky seam.

across the front of the frame from the right corner to the left corner. Cut the edge of the fox edge with the steel blade where it hits the end of the left corner. Staple the fox edge to each side of the frame, turning the seat as you go (A). Cut the fox edge with a steel blade when you reach each corner. If your frame has cutouts for the legs, cut a piece of fox edge to fit around them and staple it so that the entire rim of the frame has a sturdy edge. Place the frame burlap side up on a work surface. Roll the fox edge slightly toward the center of the frame and spray both the underside of the fox edge and the frame with a single coat of 74 adhesive. Wait 3 to 5 minutes for the glue to become tacky, then press down on the fox edge to adhere it to the frame. Set aside (B).

6. Place the frame burlap side down on the foam. Using a permanent marker, trace around the frame, adding ½" (13mm) all the way around. Cut the foam (see Cutting Foam, page 192). Because the foam sits inside the fox edge, trim the edges of the foam into a slope with the height of the fox edge as the lowest height of the slope. The side with the smallest surface area is the bottom.

NOTE | **Measuring Hides**

Leather is sold by the skin and measured by the square foot (square meter). This can be a bit deceiving, since a skin comes in the shape of the animal and the measure is taken where the skin is the widest and the longest. In general, 18 sq ft (5.5 sq m) of leather is roughly equivalent to 1 yd (91cm). The average skin is about 60 sq ft (5.6 sq m), or 3¾ yd (3.4m), far more than you need to cover a chair this size. Smaller skins from small animals are available, but I recommend looking for pieces or remnants of larger skins first (see Resources, page 200).

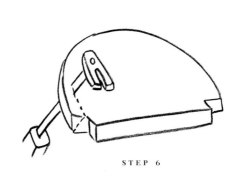

STEP 5(B)

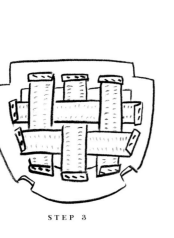

STEP 3

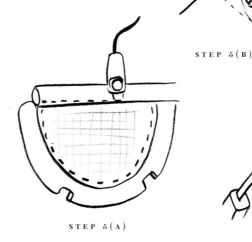

STEP 5(A)

STEP 6

Attach the Foam to the Frame

7. To affix the foam, spray 74 adhesive all over the burlap, on the inside rim, on the top edge of the fox edge, and all over the bottom and sides of the foam. Wait 3 to 5 minutes for the glue to get tacky, then set the foam, adhesive side down, inside the fox edge rim, and press down and around the rim to adhere.

8. Wrap the top and sides of the seat with Dacron. With the front of the frame facing you, staple the Dacron to frame using the Four-Point Stapling Technique. Trim away the excess Dacron, using the frame as your guide and reserving the trimmings to stuff into the seat corners after pulling the leather cover over it. Set the seat aside.

Cut the Seat Top and Border

9. To cut out the seat, place the leather right side up on a work surface. Lay the seat frame top side down on the leather. Using school chalk, trace around the frame, adding ½" (13mm) all the way around for the seam allowance. Cut along the chalk line. Set aside.

10. To determine how wide a border to cut, add 3½" (9cm) (a 3" [7.5cm] allowance for stapling to the underside of the chair and one ½" [13mm] seam allowance) to the height of the seat before you stripped it of its foam and fabric. Since our seat pad was 2" (5cm) tall, our border was 5½" (14cm) wide.

For the length of the border, add 5" (12.5cm) to the perimeter of the frame. The perimeter of our chair was 82" (208cm). Using a metal yardstick and school chalk, mark the dimensions of the border on the right side of the leather. Cut along the chalk lines. Set aside.

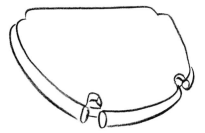

STEP 7

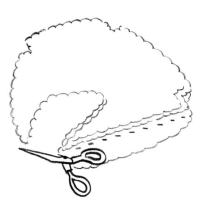

STEP 8

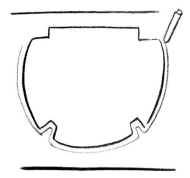

STEP 9

Sew the Welting to the Seat Top

11. If you're using welting, attach it by first folding the seat top in half lengthwise. Make a notch at the fold on the front and back of the seat. Fold the length of welting in half crosswise. Make a notch at the fold on the raw edge. Line up the notches on the welting and the front of the seat and pin the welting to the right side of the leather, raw edges together. Beginning at the front notch, machine-stitch the pieces together with a ½" (13mm) seam allowance until you reach the notch on the back of the seat. The sewing machine's foot will sit on the welting as you push the fabric through. Stop stitching ½" (13mm) from the corner, leaving

STEP 12

the needle in the leather. Cut into the leather to within ⅛" (3mm) of the thread, placing your scissors at an angle to the machine needle. Raise the presser foot, pivot the fabric 90 degrees around the needle, then sew the next side.

If your seat has a curved edge, hold your scissors perpendicular to the welting and snip every ½" (13mm) of the raw edge of the welting along the curved edge to within ⅛" (3mm) of the cord so it gives a little, and cut into the leather every ½" (13mm) to within ⅛" (3mm) of the seam.

Turn the piece over, wrong side up, and beginning at the front notch again, machine-stitch the remaining welting until you reach the back notch.

12. To join the welting, cut open 4" (10cm) of the welting at both ends using a seam ripper. Lay the canvas out flat, with one piece overlapping the other. Trim the cords on an angle to meet. Fold down one welting strip over the cord. Fold in 1" (2.5cm) on the other welting strip and fold it down over the cord. Make a notch on the canvas 1½" (3.8cm) where the welting meets. Line up the notches and machine-stitch together. The welting should sit flush against the seat cover. Sew the joined welting onto the seat cover.

Sew the Border to the Seat Top

13. To attach the border to the seat, line up the notch on the border with the notch on the front of the seat, right sides together. Beginning at the notch, machine-stitch the pieces together with a ½" (13mm) seam allowance until you reach the back notch. As you approach a corner, stop stitching ½" (13mm) from the corner. Using scissors held at an angle to the machine needle, cut the fabric to within ⅛" (3mm) of the thread. Pivot the fabric to make the corner. Stop stitching within 3" (7.5cm) of the back notch. Turn the seat over, with the wrong side up, and repeat on the other side to within 3" (7.5cm) of the back notch. Machine-stitch the ends of the border, right sides together, with a ½" (13mm) seam allowance. Press the seam open and sew the rest of the border to the seat with a ½" (13mm) seam allowance.

Attach the Seat Cover to the Padded Frame

14. Fit the seat cover over the frame. With the seat cover wrong side out, place it over the top of the frame, aligning the corners. Pull the cover over the frame, one corner at a time, beginning with the two front corners. Using a regulator as you go (see page 178), pull each corner taut so that the corners are tight. Shred the reserved Dacron and stuff each corner with a half-dollar–sized piece to make the corners crisp.

15. Fasten the cover to the frame. With the seat resting on its side, pull the leather taut and temporarily tack it in place in each corner. Cut the leather at each corner to within ¼" (6mm) of the edge of the frame so that the leather overlaps and lays flat in the corners. Staple the leather to the underside of the chair, measuring the border as you go to make sure it's the same height all the way around the chair. Using the Four-Point Tacking and Stapling Technique (page 189), staple around the entire frame, removing the tacks as you go.

Finishing

16. Place the box seat bottom side up on a work surface. Lay the cambric over it. Cut the cambric so that it overhangs the frame by 1" (2.5cm). Staple it to the frame, starting with the Four-Point Tacking and Stapling Technique (page 189) about 1" (2.5cm) from the outside edge so that all the staples underneath the cambric are covered. Once these 4 staples are in place, staple around the entire frame, snipping the corners at an angle as you did with the leather so that the fabric lays flat.

17. Attach the box seat to the chair. Place the seat on the chair and fasten on the underside with screws in each corner.

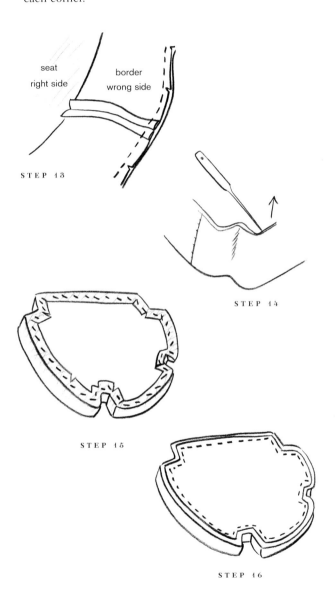

seat
right side

border
wrong side

STEP 13

STEP 14

STEP 15

STEP 16

DANISH *modern* CHAIR

THIS IS USUALLY THE KIND OF PROJECT my beginning students want to embark on the first time they attend my classes. It makes sense, since the payoff is so rewarding. It also makes sense because, like a well-written novel or beautifully prepared meal, the usually vast experience of the person behind it makes the results look effortless. So, instead of beginning with an advanced project, I first like to make sure students are adept at such essential techniques as measuring, cutting, stretching webbing, rolling edges, tacking, stapling, and smoothing fabric. In other words, beginning your foray into upholstery with a piece like this is a bit like wanting a PhD before you do the undergraduate work.

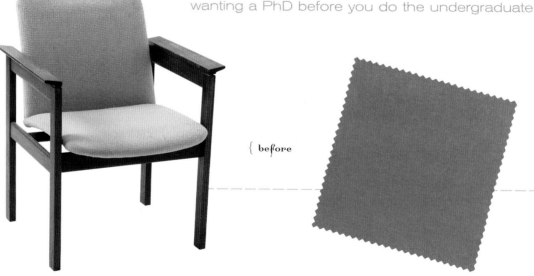

{ before

- ½ yd (46cm) burlap
- 27" (68.5cm) square piece 1½" (3.8cm) LX45 blue foam
- Electric kitchen knife or hacksaw blade
- 74 adhesive
- 2 yd (1.8m) ½" (13mm) Dacron
- 2 yd (1.8m) upholstery fabric
- 1 yd (91cm) cambric
- 3 yd (2.75m) curve ease (metal tacking strips)
- 1 yd (91cm) muslin
- ½" (13mm) wide masking tape
- Rubber mallet
- Basic upholstery tools (See page 15)

FINISHED MEASUREMENTS

All materials are for a chair with 2 frames, each 17" (43cm) square. Adjust according to the size of your piece.

Prepare the Frames

1. Strip the frames of all fabric, batting, and foam. Remove all nails and staples. Use a wire brush to scrape the surface clean of any glue.

2. Place the seat frame on a work surface, top side up. To cover the springs or webbing, lay a piece of burlap over them. Staple it to the frame using the Four-Point Tacking and Stapling Technique (page 189), shooting the staples on an angle. Create a finished edge by turning the burlap onto itself and stapling it to the frame, shooting the staples in straight and close together. Trim the excess burlap.

3. Place the seat frame top side down on the foam and, using a permanent marker, trace around the frame, adding ½" (13mm) all the way around. Cut the foam (see Cutting Foam, page 192).

Attach the Foam to the Frames

4. Spray the burlap, seat frame, and one side and all edges of the foam with 74 adhesive spray. Wait 3 to 5 minutes for theglue to become tacky, then place the foam glue side down on the burlap and press to adhere. Tuck the edges of the foam under to make a rolled edge (See Making a Rolled Edge, page 193). When rolling the back and bottom of the seat and back, roll onto the top of the frame rather than to the edge in order to leave room for the pieces to fit together.

<<< TECHNIQUE TIP

Curve ease, a flexible metal tacking strip, attaches fabric panels invisibly on curved pieces. For furniture with rounded corners, such as a camel back sofa, staple curve ease all the way along the top and down the sides of the piece. Then tack the fabric under the frame, and push it into the curve ease on the top edge, followed by the sides. If a piece has straight lines across the top, use tacking strip on the top of the frame and run the curve ease down the sides. First attach the fabric on the top edge using the tacking strips, then secure the panel under the frame, then work the sides into the curve ease.

GOING GREEN

The movement toward using environmentally friendly products has been steadily gaining traction in the past few years, and the world of upholstery has not been immune. As evidence, television shows devoted to green architecture, decorating, and living are launching everywhere. Whether it's the Al Gore effect or the general trendiness of "going green," furniture and textile companies are making efforts to offer environmentally-friendly materials.

To make your version of the projects in this book environmentally friendly, I recommend the following materials, which I have used to upholster pieces for clients and decorators alike:

- Natural latex foam to replace LX foam and white foam
- Kapok or natural wool to replace shredded Dacron
- Latex glue to replace 313 and 74 adhesives
- #33 cotton or natural wool to replace Dacron. Lay a sheet of #33 cotton fiber or wool between two pieces of muslin, and quilt it by sewing lines about ten inches (25cm) apart, similar to the way a down comforter is quilted.

Some products are environmentally friendly without being advertised as such: Jute webbing and burlap, for example, are both made from hemp.

In this book I encourage you to reupholster existing frames whenever possible, which is of course a form of recycling. But when building a frame from scratch, such as in the Custom-Built Cornice (page 72) and Three-Panel Folding Screen (page 126), consider purchasing recycled or sustainably harvested wood instead of visiting the lumber yard.

Using eco-friendly materials may be more expensive at the moment, but only because they are not yet being mass-produced on a scale that would make them more cost effective. As more customers move toward a greener lifestyle and start requesting those products, they will become more affordable. Eventually, going green will be good for the environment *and* your budget.

5. Cover the foam with Dacron. Staple it to the front and sides of the frame at the outside bottom edge using the Four-Point Tacking and Stapling Technique (page 189). At the back of the frame, staple it where the foam meets the frame. Trim the excess Dacron.

6. Repeat steps 1–4 for the seat back.

Measure and Cut the Fabric

7. To determine the dimensions of the seat, the front of the chair back, and the back of the chair back panels, measure the width and length of each and add 2" (5 cm) to all sides. For our seat, the seat and the front of the chair back panels were each 21" (53.5cm) square, and the back of the chair back panel was 22" x 24" (56cm x 61cm).

Measure, mark, and cut these panels from the upholstery fabric. Label the panels on their wrong sides.

Staple the Fabric to the Chair Seat

8. To cover the seat, drape the fabric over the padded frame, making sure the pile on the fabric brushes forward, if applicable. Because these frames are concave, the method for stapling the fabric to the frame is slightly different from that of the standard Four-Point Tacking and Stapling Technique on page 189. Wrap the fabric around the frame and staple on the underside at the halfway point of each

side, beginning in the front, followed by the back and the sides. Next, staple the fabric from front to back, alternating sides with every staple and constantly smoothing the fabric. Working your way out to the sides, remember to keep the tension of the fabric consistent. Staple the sides in the same manner. Wrap the corners, tucking the side under and pulling the front fabric over it like an envelope.

NOTE

This Danish modern chair was in excellent condition when it came into my shop—it is made from solid wood in which there were no cracks. The frame was a bit loose, but this was easy to fix with wood glue.

This chair happens to have springs—if yours has jute webbing, assess the condition of the jute and replace if necessary, or if it has nothing at all, add jute webbing to the empty frame following the instructions for Attaching Webbing to a Frame (page 190).

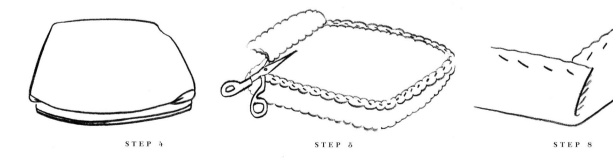

STEP 4   STEP 5   STEP 8

9. With the seat top side down, drape a piece of cambric over the frame. Trim to the dimensions of the frame. Turn the edges under and staple to the frame using the Four-Point Tacking and Stapling Technique (page 189).

Staple the Fabric to the Chair Back

10. To cover the back of the chair back, staple a continuous piece of curve ease all the way around the frame, hole side down, ¼" (6mm) (see the tip on page 172) in from the edge. Cover the strip with the masking tape.

11. Drape a piece of muslin over the back side of the chair back and trim to within the curve ease. Staple the muslin to the frame just inside the raw edge of the fabric, using the Four-Point Tacking and Stapling Technique (page 189). Fold the muslin onto itself and staple again. Trim the excess.

12. Drape a piece of the Dacron over the muslin so that it hangs over the curve ease. Staple it to the frame along the inside edge of the curve ease using the Four-Point Tacking and Stapling Technique (page 189). Trim the excess.

13. To attach the outside back, fold ½" (13mm) of the bottom edge under and staple along the bottom, stopping just short of either edge (A). Pin the top edge of the fabric along the inside back. Using school chalk, trace around the outside edge of the curve ease, feeling for the strip with your hands. Trim the fabric to within ½" (13mm) of the chalk line (B). Using a regulator, tuck the raw edge of the fabric into the curve ease, beginning at the top center and moving to the right, all the way around and down to the bottom (C). Repeat on the left-hand side, tucking the corners under as above. Using a rubber mallet, hammer the teeth of the curve ease closed.

Finishing

14. Refasten the seat and back to the chair frame.

Congratulations: You've passed an advanced test in upholstery!

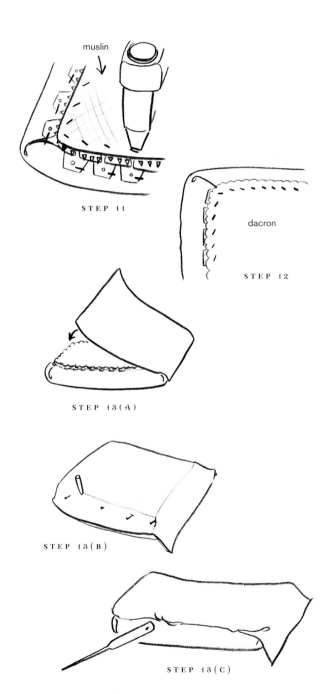

muslin

STEP 11

dacron

STEP 12

STEP 13(A)

STEP 13(B)

STEP 13(C)

The Language of Upholstery: *Essential Tools and Terms*

Stripping and Upholstery Tools

Awl: Makes fast work of lifting staples

Electric or air-powered staple gun:

Used to attach materials to a frame; it's essential that the staple gun has at least a 1½" (4cm) long nose.

Hot glue gun: Used to attach trim in certain projects in this book

Gooseneck webbing stretcher: Indispensable for affixing webbing to a frame, this lever-like tool allows you to pull the webbing taut with one hand while using the other to staple the webbing to the frame.

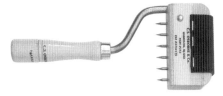

Magnetic tacking hammer: One end is magnetized to hold an upholstery tack; the other end is solid to hammer in the tack, leaving one hand free to hold the fabric.

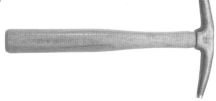

Nylon-tipped tacking hammer: Used to hammer decorative nails; the nylon tip protects the nail from dents.

Pincers: Used to remove the staple or tacks after they are lifted by the awl or staple remover. Also referred to as flush-cut or diagonal cutting nippers. At the hardware store they're sold as 7" (18cm) diagonal pliers.

Regulator: A multipurpose tool that is flat with a rounded edge on one end and sharp and pointed on the other. The pointed end is used to tuck fabric into curve ease (see page 184) while the flat end is used to make crisp folds on corners.

Rubber mallet: Used to close curve ease (see page 184)

Staple remover: Used to lift upholstery tacks

Measuring, Marking, and Cutting Tools

Dressmaker's tape measure: Used to measure upholstered pieces that are not flat, such as a seat with a rolled edge

Flexible metal yardstick: Used for marking dimensions on fabric before cutting out patterns

Heavy-duty shears: Used *only* for cutting upholstery fabric. Avoid using them for any other task that may blunt them.

Metal tape measure: A convenient measuring tool for upholstery projects because its flexibility allows you to measure around curves or corners

Razor blades: After stapling, used to cut away excess fabric as close to the staples as possible

Round curved-point needles: Used for hand-stitching seams closed and for decorative French-stitching

Plastic-head upholstery pins: Stronger than tailor's pins, these are used to hold fabric draped over a padded frame in place

Pushpins: Sometimes used to hold patterns or samples in place on top of the fabric while cutting

School chalk: Used for marking cutting lines on cambric and upholstery fabric. It's easy to wipe away if you make a mistake and need to redraw the lines. Experienced upholsterers use tailor's chalk, but it should be used only if you are confident that you are marking out the piece correctly, as it is difficult to remove.

Small shears: Used for cutting Dacron and other padding as well as excess fabric while upholstering

Straight single round-point needle: Used to stitch through fabric and underlying layers of padding to secure it to a foundation. Often used with tufting twine (see the Biscuit Tufted Bench, page 132). Can also be used to sew on buttons.

Dressmaker's pins: Used to secure patterns to fabric for cutting, and to hold fabric together before machine-stitching. They are sometimes called straight pins.

Sewing Terms and Tools

Sewing Machine: All of the projects in this book can be made with a home sewing machine. However, should you wish to graduate to thicker fabrics such as mohair, leather, velvet, or vinyl, an industrial sewing machine will open up a new world of fabric.

Home sewing machine

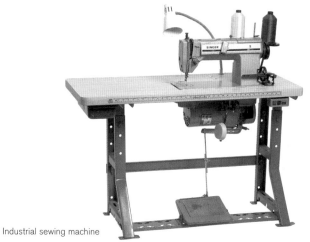

Industrial sewing machine

Seam ripper: A small, pointed tool used for unpicking stitches or whenever a line of stitching needs to be removed.

Selvedge: The long, finished edge on either side of a roll of fabric (see the illustration on page 187)

Straight-stitch foot: Used on a sewing machine for stitching all seams that do not have welting ¼" (6mm)

Topstitch guide foot: A two-part sewing machine foot in which one toe is higher than the other. The lower side sits against the edge of the fabric, making it easy to topstitch close to it and stitch a straight line.

Welting: A cord-like decorative trim used in the Throw Pillow with Welting (page 46); also called piping. Learn how to make your own on page 49.

Welting foot: A deep groove on the bottom of this foot accommodates welting, allowing the fabric to slide smoothly underneath the foot to prevent puckering.

Zipper foot: Essential for stitching zippers, this sewing machine foot allows you to work as closely as possible to the teeth of the zipper.

Padding Material

Dacron: A layer of padding between the foam and the fabric that prevents the fabric from rubbing against the foam, which can degrade the foam. In this book, unless a project specifically calls for shredded Dacron, which is used to stuff into corners to create tight, crisp angles, ½" (13mm) Dacron is meant.

Shredded Dacron

½" Dacron

Feather blend: Foam chips mixed with feathers, mainly used for lumbar pillows and arm bolsters. It is denser and firmer than down and feathers.

LX blue foam: A high-resiliency foam used for seat cushions, back cushions, and for padding the body. Available in many thicknesses and several densities. This foam is fire retardant, whereas white foam is not.

LX45 is a hard-density foam used in projects for which the foam is 2" thick (5cm) or less. **LX35,** a medium-density foam, is used in projects for which the foam is thicker than 2" (5cm).

White foam: The price difference between this and blue foam is minimal, but blue foam is a better, longer lasting foam.

Foundation Material

Burlap: A loosely woven fabric used to cover webbing as added support

Cambric: Fastened to the underside of upholstered pieces to give them a finished look; it is also used to make patterns.

Plastic webbing: Used instead of jute webbing on such pieces as folding screens, onto which no weight is applied

Fox edge: A cotton- or paper-stuffed burlap tube that is attached to a frame to pad it

Jute webbing: A webbing woven from natural fibers, used on pieces pressure will be applied to, such as chair seats

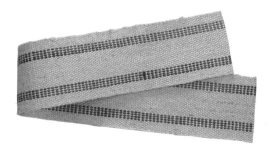

Window Treatment Tools and Fabrics

Brass-plated sew-on rings: Tiny circlets hand-stitched to the Roman shade along its length and used for threading the lift cord

Buckram: A 3–6" (7.5–15cm) stiff, polyester, nonadhesive tape that stiffens the top of drapes

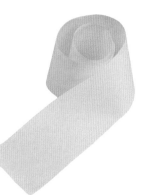

Cord cleat: Used for taking up the slack of the excess cord on Roman shades

Cord drop: Decorative piece placed at the ends of the lift cords in a Roman shade

Drapery lining: Lightweight fabric, usually in a neutral color, used to line the back of draperies, valances, and Roman shades

Drapery pins: Inserted into the back of the drapery to hold it to the rings on the rod

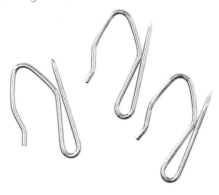

Lift cord: Threaded through the rings of a Roman shade for raising and lowering

Microscrew eyes: Screwed into the header on a Roman shade and used for threading the lift cord through

Threads and Twines

Choose the thickest and strongest thread possible for use in your sewing machine—remember, your body weight will be pulling at these seams.

#18 nylon hand-stitching thread: Available in many colors, it fits through the head of the curved needles that are used for hand-stitching

Bonded 69 nylon machine thread: Used in industrial sewing machines and for hand-stitching seams closed, as in the Lined Round Tablecloth (page 32)

Tufting twine: Thick nylon twine used to create a tufted surface on plain fabric or to sew buttons

Tacks, Staples, and Zippers

Curve ease: A flexible metal tacking strip used on curved pieces, when tacking is not possible to attach fabric panels invisibly

Decorative nails: An embellishment on many upholstered pieces, these are available in dozens of styles and materials, including nickel, Z, French, and old brass, to name a few.

#7¾" (19mm) staples: Used when stapling webbing to a frame (equivalent to #14 tacks)

#7½" (13mm) staples: Used when stapling a tacking strip or curve ease to a frame (equivalent to #4 tacks)

#7¼" (6mm) upholstery staples: Used to staple fabric to a frame (equivalent to #3 tacks)

#3, #4, and #14 tacks: Used in place of staples on upholstered pieces for attaching fabric, tacking strip, curve ease, or webbing to a frame

Nickel

old brass

#4

#14

#3

Nylon zippers: The continuous version can be cut to size and fitted with a zipper pull. Those sold in predetermined lengths with the zipper pull attached are also fine to use.

Tacking strip: Cardboard stripping used to achieve a straight, crisp edge or line where two upholstered fabric pieces meet

Adhesives

74 adhesive: Heavy-duty spray used in this book to secure blue foam to burlap-covered webbing and Dacron, to make a rolled edge, and to glue pieces of foam together. Becomes tacky in 3–5 minutes.

313 adhesive: A lightweight spray used to glue foam to a flat surface and to glue Dacron to foam. Becomes tacky in 1–2 minutes.

½" (13mm) masking tape: Used to cover curve ease and other metal tacking strips before tucking fabric into them

Fringe adhesive: A fabric glue that dries clear. Used to finish the knots on the back of the Relaxed Roman Shade.

Upholstery Techniques 101

Measure Twice, Cut Once: Basic Methods of Measuring and Cutting Fabrics

Length is the primary measurement to establish when figuring out your fabric's dimensions, since most upholstery fabric widths are set sizes, generally 48" (122cm) and 54" (137cm). Other materials, such as cambric, linings, and lightweight fabrics that you may choose to use for pillows, vary in width.

Every roll of fabric contains four edges. The rolled edge is wrapped around the cardboard tubing. The cut edge is where the manufacturer has cut it, on the opposite end of the rolled edge. The selvedges run down the length of the fabric on both sides. In directions referring to patterned or piled fabric, you may come across the term *up the roll*, which describes fabrics in which the top of the pattern or pile hits at the rolled or cut edge. Other fabrics are *railroaded*, which means the top of the pattern or pile of the fabric hits at the selvedge. In other words, when railroaded fabric is laid out on a work surface with the cut edge to your left and the roll to your right, the pattern or pile is upright, not sideways. Both railroaded fabrics and those running up the roll can be used for the projects in this book, but when reupholstering a large piece such as a sofa, choose a railroaded fabric so that you can cut the piece as wide as you need and avoid visible seams from sewing together multiple pieces of fabric.

NOTE: In this book, you'll come across the terms "crosswise" and "lengthwise" when asked to fold pieces to cut them in half or notch the centers. When folding

crosswise, fold so that the short ends come together; fold lengthwise by placing the long ends together.

To take accurate measurements, it is essential to always have on hand a cloth tape measure, a metal yardstick, a ruler, and a square. Here are my basic guidelines on how to measure and cut accurately:

1. Take careful measurements of every part of the furniture piece before stripping it. This includes the finished height of the cushions from the floor up.

2. Make a list of every fabric piece needed, and write the measurements in length x width; the length is always the up-and-down or front-to-back measurement, whereas the width is the side-to-side measurement. Add the necessary allowances: As a general rule of thumb, add 2" (5cm) anywhere the fabric is stapled or tacked. Always measure from stapled edge to stapled edge or stapled edge to sewn edge—whatever the case may be—and then add 2" (5cm). Use a dressmaker's tape measure, and when measuring the inside back and arms of a sofa or chair, push it down into the edges of the seat frame. Whenever possible, use the old fabric as your pattern; otherwise, measure and mark the cambric in all dimensions to make a pattern. Use school chalk to label each pattern piece.

3. Determine how much fabric to buy by making a diagram on a piece of muslin or cambric, making note of the width of the roll. Add a ½ yd (46cm) for flexibility and roughly another 1 yd (91cm) if you're using fabric with a large pattern so that you can match it up. A rule of thumb for determining patterned fabric yardage: Add the length of the

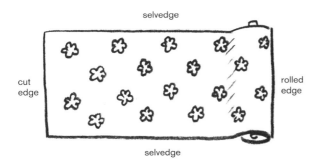

selvedge

cut edge

rolled edge

selvedge

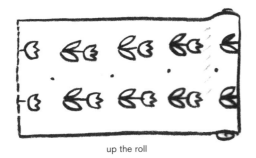

up the roll

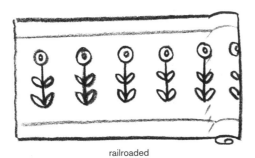

railroaded

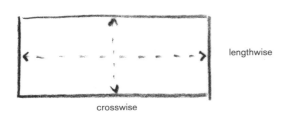

lengthwise

crosswise

pattern repeat to the length of the cut. For example, if the length the pattern calls for is 25" (63.5cm) and the pattern repeat is 25" (63.5cm), then the length of fabric you need to match up the pattern is 50" (127cm).

4. Trim the selvedges and end of the fabric so that it is square. Use a carpenter's square or align a metal yardstick along the pattern repeat markings on the selvedges to keep your cut square.

5. Pin the patterns to the right side of the fabric. Using heavy-duty scissors, cut out as directed in the project, keeping the lower blade of the scissors on the work surface at all times and maintaining the tension of the fabric with your other hand. Mark the wrong side of each cut piece of fabric with school chalk. Leave the patterns pinned to the fabric until ready to use—this makes it easy to identify each piece.

Stripping Furniture

All instructions for the reupholstery projects in this book are based on furniture pieces that need to be stripped from the frame. Removing the old upholstery, padding, and foundation materials from furniture requires just as careful and thorough attention as putting it back on. Resist the urge to dismantle the piece willy-nilly; the following preparation steps will produce the a far better outcome.

MATERIALS

Camera

Staple remover and awl

Pincers

School chalk

1. Take pictures. Before I remove a single tack, staple, or piece of fabric from furniture I am reupholstering, I take digital pictures of the piece intact as well as after stripping the fabric and padding from it. I'm especially careful to

document unusual details that the client wants reproduced exactly, such as a specific type of pleating on the skirt. These images serve as a historical blueprint and an invaluable reference as you re-cover a piece.

2. Prepare your workspace. When you're ready to begin stripping your furniture, place it at waist level on a clean work surface. Upholstering can be quite physically challenging, especially to your back and knees, if you are working with a piece on the floor or at an improper height. A large piece of plywood and two sawhorses are all you need to create a makeshift workstation.

3. Remove and record every piece of fabric. Once you've cleared ample space for working, begin by removing the upholstery in the reverse order that it was attached to the frame. For sofas and chairs, this generally means starting with the skirt, if there is one, then moving on to the outside back and arms, followed by the inside back and arms. As you remove each piece, label it with school chalk and take note of how it was affixed to another piece of fabric or the frame: Was it machine-stitched, hand-stitched, stapled or tacked, or gripped with tacking strip? In some instances, you will find a second layer of upholstery under the top layer—remove it, too.

4. Strip the padding and foundation. In general, if a piece of furniture requires reupholstering, the materials supporting the fabric—muslin, Dacron, foam, and webbing, for example—usually need replacing, too. Remember to remove all tacks, nails, and staples. I find that a staple remover works best for removing tacks. Using the pincers, hammer it under the tack and pry it upward and out. Use the awl the same way to remove staples. The frame should be completely clean before you proceed—use a wire brush to remove old glue, if necessary.

Four-Point Tacking and Stapling Technique

Every time you use tacks or staples to fasten anything—whether it's burlap, muslin, Dacron, upholstery fabric, or cambric—to a frame, use this method for doing so. It prevents improper stretching, helps to keep the fabric aligned, and aids in achieving consistent tension in the fabric—the key to a professional-looking upholstery job. The instructions for each project specify tacks or staples, or sometimes both: Many projects, such as the Bench with Decorative Nails (page 66) suggest using tacks to temporarily pin the fabric to the frame before stapling it.

MATERIALS

Staple gun or tacking hammer
Upholstery tacks

1. With the front of the frame facing you and the fabric positioned as directed in the project's instructions, hammer the upholstery tack through the fabric into the center front of the frame. Pull and smooth the fabric gently so that it is taut but doesn't pucker, and hammer a tack through the fabric into the center back of the frame. Pull and smooth again, then hammer a third tack through the fabric into the center right-hand side of the frame, followed by the center left, making sure to keep the weave straight and the design motifs aligned. This process is the same when shooting staples instead of hammering upholstery tacks.

2. Once you've tacked or stapled each side in the center, tack (or staple) the corners, if there are any, beginning with the back right-hand corner and working in a clockwise direction.

3. Finish tacking or stapling the fabric to each side, beginning to the right of the first tack and spacing the tacks ⅛" (3mm) apart. Work your way counterclockwise around the frame until you reach the first tack or staple, making sure to keep the tension consistent as you work.

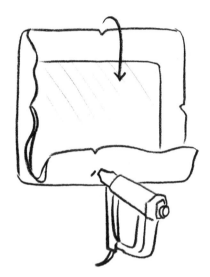

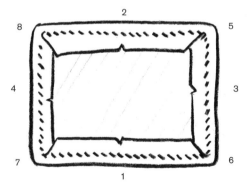

Attaching Webbing to a Frame

For all of my jobs, I prefer to use staples rather than upholstery tacks for securing webbing to a frame. Old-school upholsterers and purists may disagree with my choice, but the truth is, stapling goes much faster and the results are exactly the same, with less damage to old frames.

Hold the stapler flush against the material and the frame, at a 45-degree angle from the edge so that the staples go into the frame on an angle. This prevents the webbing from ripping under pressure.

MATERIALS

School chalk

Jute or plastic webbing

Staple gun

7 ¾" (2cm) staples

Webbing stretcher

Tacking hammer

#14 tacks

1. Place the frame top side up on a work surface. Determine the number and spacing of strips of webbing so that they are an equal distance apart. I like to space mine about 1" (2.5cm) apart. Mark the centers of the front and back of the frame with the school chalk. Line up the center of the full length of webbing with the back chalk mark if using an odd number of strips, or line up the edge of the strip with the center mark if using an even number of strips. With 1½" (3.8cm) of webbing hanging over the edge of the frame, staple one end of the strip to the inside edge of the back of the frame, stapling on an angle and using the staple marks from the old webbing as your guide. Fold back the overhanging webbing onto itself and staple on an angle. Trim the raw edge to within ⅛" (3mm) of the staples.

2. With the webbing stretcher in one hand, grab the webbing with the teeth of the stretcher and pull the webbing over the front of the frame, and with the other hand, pull the webbing taut and staple it at an angle to

the inside edge of the frame. Cut the webbing 1½"
(3.8cm) from the staples. Fold the loose end back onto the
webbing and staple on an angle. Trim the raw edge to
within ⅛" (3mm) of the staples.

3. Repeat, moving across the frame and spacing the
webbing strips at an equal distance from one another.
Make sure to stretch all strips equally taut. Using a tacking
hammer, gently hammer the staples into the frame.

4. Mark the centers of the sides of the frame with school
chalk. Determine the number and spacing of strips of
webbing so that they are an equal distance apart. Line up
the center of the full length of webbing with the back
chalk mark if using an odd number of strips, or line up
the edge of the strip with the chalk mark if using an even
number of strips.

5. Working from side to side, weave the webbing over and
under the attached strips and staple the starting end as
you did the front-to-back strips. Attach the remaining
strips, reversing the weave pattern of the adjacent strips.

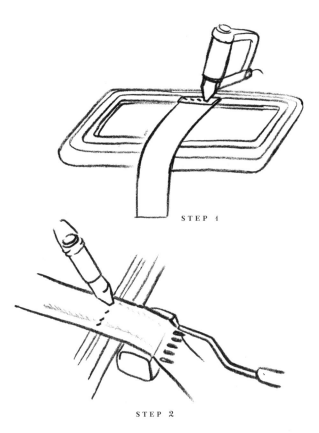

STEP 1

STEP 2

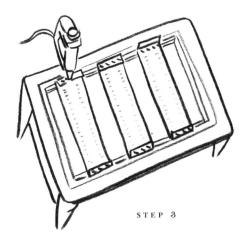

STEP 3

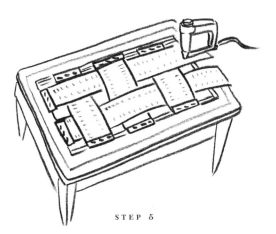

STEP 5

Cutting Foam

A foam cutter—an electric saw with a vertical blade and flat
base—is used professionally to cut high-density foams.
However, for all of the projects in this book, an electric
kitchen knife or hacksaw blade can be used instead of a
foam cutter, as long as you keep it vertical as you cut. First
trace your cutting shape onto the foam with a permanent
marker, then cut out using the electric knife or hacksaw blade.
Again, be sure to keep the tool upright so that the foam's edge
is perfectly vertical after cutting.

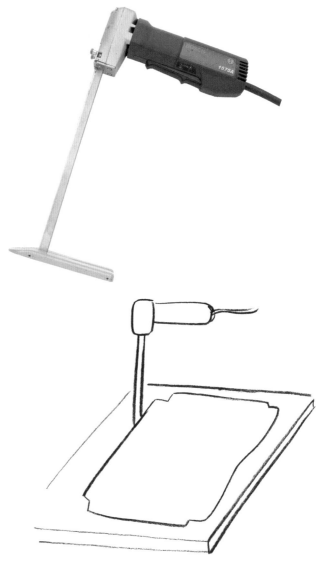

Making a Rolled Edge

A rolled edge is typically found on dining chairs and upholstered stools.

MATERIALS

Foam in thickness and density as directed in project instructions

74 adhesive

Regulator

1. After the foam is glued to the frame, spray the side of the foam with 74 adhesive where you plan to begin. If the foam is 1" (2.5cm) thick or more, spray only the top half of the side. Experienced upholsterers often spray all sides at once, but the glue may dry on the other edges before the novice will get around to rolling them.

2. Beginning at the center of one side of the frame's edges (or anywhere if the frame is round or oval) tuck the bottom edge of the foam under with the regulator and, using the other hand, pull the top edge of the foam over the bottom edge, pressing it firmly onto the frame. Work this way to the corner, then return to the center and tuck and pull to the opposite corner. Repeat on the remaining sides.

STEP 2

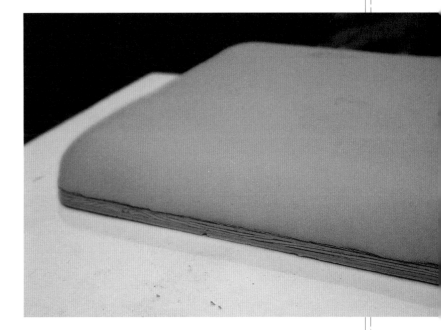

Sewing Basics

The projects in this book were designed to be stitched using a home sewing machine. The following are some common stitch techniques used for the projects in this book.

Backstitch: When beginning or ending a line of machine-stitching, the reverse function on the sewing machine is used to double back on the preceding stitch. This reinforces the stitching and ensures it does not unravel. All lines of stitching should be backstitched when sewing the projects in this book. When sewing a zipper, remember to backstitch beyond both ends 2" (5cm) so that the ends of the zipper do not slip out of the pillow or cushion.

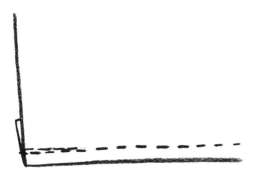

Hand-stitch: For some projects, I instruct you to hand-stitch seams closed, as in the Lined Round Tablecloth (page 32), Knife-Edged Settee Pad (page 90), and the French-Stitched Window Seat (page 138). By using the following method, hand-stitched seams are undistinguishable from their machine-sewn counterparts. A 3½" (9cm) curved needle and machine-stitching thread are all you need for the projects on the following pages. If you are using lightweight fabrics, use a smaller, thinner needle.

1. Tuck the fabric under ½" (13mm), or the stated seam allowance, and pin. Thread the curved needle with machine-stitching thread, tying a slipknot on the long end. Coming up through the back of the fabric, make a ¼" (6mm) stitch on one side of the seam as close as possible to the edge where the two pieces of fabric meet. Pull the thread through.

2. Make the next stitch on the other side of the seam directly opposite to where the needle exited on the last stitch.

3. Again, switch to the opposite side for the next stitch, and continue stitching in this manner, taking care to keep the tension on the thread consistent.

4. When the seam is entirely stitched closed, wrap the thread around the needle once or twice and make a tiny stitch into the fabric, holding the thread firmly near the point at which you inserted the stitch. Pull the needle back toward you to produce a knot that will secure your stitches.

Saddle stitch: Typically, this is topstitching using a thread contrasting in color with the fabric, used primarily as ornament. The saddle stitch used in the Saddle-Stitched Bolster (page 54) contains two lines of stitching: The seam between the disk and the body of the bolster is pressed open and the edge of both the body and the disc is topstitched.

Topstitch: To sew a line of stitches on the face side of a project, next to a seam. Used in the Embellished Table Runner (page 26).

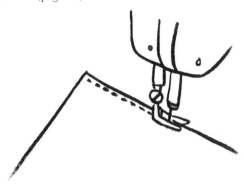

Zigzag stitch: A stitch function on almost all home sewing machines; commonly used to finish edges to prevent fraying

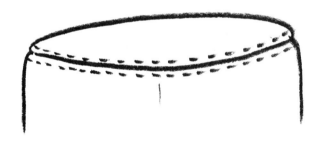

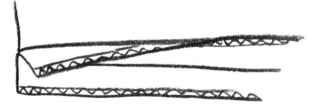

Fabric Yardage Guide

Here is a visual guide to help you determine fabric yardage amounts when reupholstering your existing sofas and chairs. If you're using patterned fabric, remember to increase the fabric by approximately 10 to 20 percent in order to match up the pattern.

9 YARDS

24 YARDS

9 YARDS

8 YARDS

8 YARDS

8 YARDS

14 YARDS

7–8 YARDS

26 YARDS

6 YARDS

10 YARDS

12–15 YARDS

4 YARDS

14–16 YARDS

12–14 YARDS

9 YARDS

20 YARDS

4 YARDS

20 YARDS

16–18 YARDS

16–18 YARDS

10–12 YARDS

8.5 YARDS

22 YARDS

6 YARDS

6 YARDS

6 YARDS

12 YARDS

6 YARDS

7–8 YARDS

24 YARDS

14 YARDS

12–14 YARDS

12–14 YARDS

9–10 YARDS

10 YARDS

26 YARDS

8 YARDS

6 YARDS

22 YARDS

6 YARDS

24 YARDS

14 YARDS

6–7.5 YARDS

6 YARDS

16–18 YARDS

9 YARDS

12–14 YARDS

6 YARDS

12–14 YARDS

9 YARDS

8 YARDS

7.5 YARDS

8 YARDS

8 YARDS

14 YARDS

18 YARDS

8 YARDS

24 YARDS

8 YARDS

16–18 YARDS

24 YARDS

Resources

The following is a list of companies who stock the upholstery tools, lumber, hardware supplies, sewing machines, and fabric needed for the projects in this book. Go to the company's website to locate the store nearest you, order online, or place an order over the phone.

Upholstery Tools and Supplies

Alan Richard Textile
40 New York Ave
Westbury, NY 11590
800-441-6248

B&M Latex Sales, Ltd.
169a High Street
Hampton Hill
Middlesex
TW12 1NL
UK
+44 (0)208 979 0457
www.bandmlatexupholstery.co.uk

C. S. Osborne & Co.
125 Jersey Street
Harrison, NJ 07029
973-483-3232
www.csosborne.com

Discount Fabrics USA
108 N. Carroll Street
Thurmont, MD 21788
877-271-2266
www.discountfabricsusacorp.com

Foam Order.com
1325 Howard Street
San Franscico, CA 94103
859-971-2531
www.foamorder.com
www.upholster.com

Handtools-UK
58 Dene Street
Dorking
Surrey
RH4 2DP
UK
+44 (0)1306 740 433
www.handtools-uk.com

Houles Paris
2 chemin de la Coudrette
F-77123 Noisy sur École
+33(0)1 60 39 62 01
www.houles.com

J. A. Milton Upholstery Supplies, Ltd.
Ellesmere Business Park
Ellesmere
Shropshire
SY12 OEW
UK
+44 (0)870 777 8934
www.jamiltonupholstery.co.uk

Perfect Fit - McDonald, Inc.
18249 Olympic Avenue S
Tukwila, WA 98188
800-652- 5202
www.perfectfit.com

PerfectProductsOnline.com
236 West Portal Avenue, #170
San Francisco, CA 94127
415-738-8601
www.perfectproductsonline.com

Rochford Supply, Inc.
1500 Washington Avenue N
Minneapolis, MN 55411
800-334-6414
www.rochfordsupply.com

Rowley Co
800-343-4542
www.rowleyco.com

Van Dyke's Restorers
PO Box 278
39771 S.D. Highway 34
Woonsocket, SD 57385
800-787-3355
www.vandykes.com

Woodworker's Supply, Inc.
800-645-9292
www.woodworker.com

Lumber Supplies

Dykes Lumber
348 West 44th Street
New York, NY 10036
212-582-1930
www.dykeslumber.com

Home Depot
www.homedepot.com

Rosenzweig Lumber
801 East 135th Street
Bronx, NY 10454
800-228-7674
www.rosenzweiglumber.com

Hardware Supplies

Ace Hardware
www.acehardware.com

Home Depot
www.homedepot.com

Sewing Machine Companies and Supplies

Jo-Ann Fabric & Craft Stores

888-739-4120
www.joann.com

Joseph Gutman Associates

120 West 25th Street
New York, NY 10001
212-243-0790

JUKI America, Inc.

500 NW 17th Street, Suite 100
Miami, FL 33126
305-594-0059
www.juki.com

Raphael Sewing

6340 St Laurent Blvd
Montreal, Quebec
Canada H2S 3C4
514-270-1537
www.raphaelsewing.com

Rubie Green
www.rubiegreen.com

Singer Sewing Company
1224 Heil Quaker Boulevard
P.O. Box 7017
LaVergne, TN 37086
1-800-4-SINGER
www.singerco.com

Vais Sewing Machine Co., Inc.
1129 Mcdonald Avenue
Brooklyn, NY 11230
718-677-6474

Fabrics

Design centers across the country offer access to many fabric companies all within one building. These centers are normally only open to designers and decorators; however, each center offers a buying service for consumers to purchase directly.

Boston Design Center
Buying Service: Designer on Call
(617-338-5062 x106)

Decorative Center (Houston)
Buying Service: Decorative Center Service (713-961-1271)

Design Center of the Americas (Dania Beach, FL)
Buying Service: Design On Call
(800-57-DCOTA)

Denver Design Center
Buying Service: Design Connection
(303-733-2455)

International Market Square (Minneapolis)
Buying Service: Design Connection
(612-338-6250)

Marketplace Design Center (Philadelphia)
Buying Service: Diane Reushel of Sapphire Interiors (215-557-0665)

Michigan Design Center (Troy, MI)
Buying Service: Designers on Call
(248-649-4772)

New York Design Center (New York City)
Buying Service: Interior Options
(212-726-9708)

D&D Building (New York City)
Buying Service: Design Professionals
(212-759-6894)

Pacific Design Center (Los Angeles)
Buying Service: Pacific Design Services
(310-657-0800)

San Francisco Design Center
Buying Service: Designers in the building (415-490-5800)

Seattle Design Center
Buying Service: The Studio
(206-762-1200 x253)

Washington Design Center (DC)
Buying Service: Dial-a-Designer
(202-646-6100)

Contributed Fabrics

The following is a list of the fabrics and trimmings used for the projects in this book, which were generously donated by various companies: Clarence House, Cowtan & Tout, Hinson & Company, Larsen, Lulu DK at Hinson & Company, M & J Trimming, Manuel Canovas, Scalamandré, and Old World Weavers.

Embellished Table Runner (page 27): Off-white silk, Trim: M&J Trimming, Geometric Jacquard in Brown/Natural

Lined Round Tablecloth (page 33): Hinson & Company, Neuville Texture in Green

Throw Pillows: Clarence House, Wool Diamond in Red, Trim: M&J Trimming, Jute Braided Cordredge in Dark Jute with Natural Tape (Throw Pillow with Welting, page 47); Cowtan & Tout, Circa in Cinnamon, No Trim (Throw Pillow with a Flange, page 51); Manuel Canovas, Jouvance in Geranium, Trim: M&J Trimming, 23MM Box Pleated Grossgrain in 173

Ecru (Throw Pillow with Box Trim, page 43)

Director's Chair (page 16): Manuel Canovas, Santiago

Bench with Decorative Nails (page 67): Old World Weavers, Figaro in Mauve/Blanc, Trim: M&J Trimming, 9MM Chromespun Grosgrain in 3/8" Ivory

Custom-Built Cornice (page 73): Larsen, Silhouette in Hazelnut, Sheer Fabric: Larsen, Continuum in Pearl

Relaxed Roman Shade (page 79): Hinson & Company, Astley Silk Stripe in French Blue

Stool with Drop-In Seat (page 85): Lulu DK at Hinson & Company, Catwalk in Sky

Knife-Edged Settee Pad (page 91): Hinson & Company, Tipper Stripe in Black/Tan, Trim: M&J Trimming, Tab Cordredge Black

Floor Lounge Cushion (page 95): Old World Weavers, Jacaranda in Mesa

Half-Skirt Slipcover (page 101): Cowtan & Tout, Pensford Stripe in Blue/Beige

Buckram-Topped Curtains (page 107): Manuel Canovas, Volange Metis in Lin

Fringed Cube-Shaped Pouf (page 113): Old World Weavers, Rosine II in Chocolat, Trim: M&J Trimming, Souffle Brush Fringe in Coffee

Boudoir Stool (page 119): Lulu DK at Hinson & Company, Tulah in Pale Blue, Trim: M&J Trimming, 8MM Rayon Pearl Cordredge in Clear Springs

Three-Panel Folding Screen (page 127): Lulu DK at Hinson & Company, Paradiso in Ocean

Biscuit-Tufted Bench (page 133): Manuel Canovas, Lafayette in Rouge Venetian

French-Stitched Window Seat (page 139): Old World Weavers, Diamonds in Raspberry Espresso

Cushioned Library Chair (page 145): black and white herring bone with z nails trim (no fabric source)

Upholstered Headboard (page 151): Lulu DK at Hinson & Company, Minerva in Crème with Blue, Trim: M&J Trimming, Imported Wool Folding Braid in Ivory

Full Slipcover (page 155): Lulu DK at Hinson & Company, Labyrinth in Dark Brown with Red

Danish Modern Chair (page 171): Cowtan & Tout, Lafayette in sage green

Acknowledgments

I'd like to thank the following people for their personal support and professional contributions. Without their help, this book would not have been possible.

Carla Glasser, Betsy Nolan Literary Agency: Carla, thanks for getting the wheel turning, and remember, there is no gray.

Kathleen Hackett: Maybe your longest journey yet, but it could not have been done without you—thanks! See you for the next one. :)

Marcus Tullis, photographer: Your positivity and patience is second-to-none and much appreciated.

Allison Tick, stylist

Stephen Antonson: I'm sure the "upholstery book" conversations were endless—thanks for hanging in there.

Ksenya Samarskaya: Hope you still have the "pouch."

Vesna Babic, Carmen Bruni, Linda Derefler, Miry Park, Paulette Smyth: Thanks for your assistance in supplying fabrics.

Fran Reilly of Story Antiques/The Antiques Showplace: I promise you will get the pieces back.

Thank you, Caryl and Kerry Swain, for the storage space, furniture, transportation, food, advice, Laura . . . the list goes on. Kerry, you are welcome for the snowboarding lessons.

Rosy Ngo, Erin Slonaker, Jen Graham, Chi Ling Moy, and everyone at Potter Craft, thanks for taking a chance on such a unique project.

Laura Swain: Where to begin? Your unconditional love and support, Jaden—the gifts you give are endless. At some point I will master bending like bamboo as well as you have.

SPECIAL THANKS
to some of The Furniture Joint staff:
Wilson Garcés and Consuelo Silva

Index